Citizenship and Social Class

PLUTO PERSPECTIVES

Series Editor Professor Robert Moore

Pluto Perspectives has created a forum for independent academics and commentators to offer sustained analytical critiques of inviduals, institutions, themes and movements on what has now come to be identified as the 'New Right'.

Already published:

The New Crusaders: Christianity and the New Right in Southern Africa
PAUL GIFFORD

Hayek and the Market
JIM TOMLINSON

Citizenship and Social Class

T.H. Marshall and Tom Bottomore

PLUTO  **PRESS**

First published 1992 by Pluto Press
345 Archway Road, London N6 5AA

www.plutobooks.com

British Library Cataloguing in Publication Data
A catalogue record for this book is available from the British
Library

Library of Congress Cataloging in Publication Data
Applied for

ISBN 9780745304779 hardback
ISBN 074530477X hardback
ISBN 9780745304762 paperback
ISBN 0745304761 paperback

Printed on Demand by Antony Rowe Ltd, Eastbourne

Contents

Foreword

It may seem perverse to include T.H. Marshall's seminal 1950 essay on citizenship in a series of books devoted to a critical analysis of the work of the New Right in the 1970s and 1980s. But if there has been one central target for the New Right it has been the idea of citizenship. None has chosen to confront Marshall's work directly but the increasing extent to which Marshall has been discussed and footnoted in the last two decades is evidence enough of his influence.

For the authoritarian New Right, of whom the Peterhouse Group and *Salisbury Review* authors would be typical, the idea of citizenship is a liberal absurdity that gives people ideas above their stations. It leads subjects to cease thinking of themselves as subjects and to believe themselves to be persons endowed with rights, rather than under the obligation to be governed. They regret the American and French revolutions, which celebrated citizenship. They regard liberalism as more dangerous than Marxism because it is less self-evidently absurd (in their view) and contains seductive ideas of individual freedom and civil rights.

For the libertarian New Right citizenship implies a body of rights that transcend and modify market relations, a central tenet of Marshall's argument. For libertarians, ranging from the Adam Smith Institute to the Institute for Economic Affairs, the state should function only to maintain the rule of law and the currency. Relations between individuals should be governed by the market, with recourse only to the law if harm is done by the market. All forms of collectivism undermine the market and when the state seeks to abrogate it by attempting to aggregate the millions of individual needs that should be mediated by the market, economic chaos and political tyranny ensue. For Marshall taming market forces was an essential precondition for a just society.

Marshall's notion of citizenship has been a leading mark in post-war sociology and social policy and its importance has grown rather than diminished in the years since *Citizenship and Social Class* was first published. It is an appropriate moment to make the original essay widely available again.

Robert Moore
Liverpool, August 1991

Preface

It has been an especial pleasure to write the complementary essay on citizenship and social class for this volume. The ideas which T.H. Marshall expounded, and the issues he raised, in his monograph of 1950 are as vital as ever today, and his writings continue to influence sociological studies in many countries. Indeed, the references to them seem to multiply as the years pass. My own work in these fields has always been influenced by my long association with him, as a colleague at the London School of Economics from 1952, then in a different way when he was the director of the Social Sciences Department in UNESCO (1956–60) while I was the executive secretary of the International Sociological Association, and finally during his very active retirement, in the early years of which he was the president of the ISA (1959–62) and also played a major part in establishing sociology at Cambridge.

In later years, when he had turned his attention mainly to more detailed issues of social welfare, in successive editions of his widely read and very influential book *Social Policy*, I again learned much from discussions with him, not least from the way in which he systematically related questions of welfare to the wider social structure in essays on welfare capitalism, the mixed economy and socialism. Looking back on his work it seems to me that it has three distinctive and admirable features. First there is the clarity and elegance of his exposition (a rare enough quality among social scientists), secondly the careful and critical way in which he analysed major social trends and matters of policy formation, and thirdly the restrained, but very apparent, expression of hopefulness about the possibility of achieving greater social justice.

Marshall himself, in a memoir on his career contributed to the *International Social Science Journal* (vol. XXV, no. 1/2, 1973) wrote of the value of sociology as part of a liberal education. His own work was a major contribution to such an education, and in a broader sense to the process of creating a more humane and civilised society. Sociologists of the present generation have still much to learn from him.

Tom Bottomore
August 1991

Part I
Citizenship and Social Class
T.H. Marshall

1. The Problem Stated with the Assistance of Alfred Marshall

The invitation to deliver these lectures[1] gave me both personal and professional pleasure. But, whereas my personal response was a sincere and modest appreciation of an honour I had no right to expect, my professional reaction was not modest at all. Sociology, it seemed to me, had every right to claim a share in this annual commemoration of Alfred Marshall, and I considered it a sign of grace that a University which has not yet accepted sociology as an inmate should nevertheless be prepared to welcome her as a visitor. It may be–and the thought is a disturbing one–that sociology is on trial here in my person. If so, I am sure I can rely on you to be scrupulously fair in your judgement, and to regard any merit you may find in my lectures as evidence of the academic value of the subject I profess, while treating everything in them that appears to you paltry, common or ill-conceived as the product of qualities peculiar to myself and not to be found in any of my colleagues.

I will not defend the relevance of my subject to the occasion by claiming Marshall as a sociologist. For, once he had deserted his first loves of metaphysics, ethics and psychology, he devoted his life to the development of economics as an independent science and to the perfection of its own special methods of investigation and analysis. He deliberately chose a path markedly different from that followed by Adam Smith and John Stuart Mill, and the mood in which he made this choice is indicated in the inaugural lecture which he delivered here in Cambridge in 1885. Speaking of Comte's belief in a unified social science, he said: 'No doubt if that existed economics would gladly find shelter under its wing. But it does not exist; it shows no signs of coming into existence. There is no use in waiting idly for it; we must do what we can with our present resources.[2] He therefore defended the autonomy and the superiority of the economic method, a superiority due mainly to its use of the measuring rod of money, which 'is so much the best measure of motives that no other can compete with it.'[3]

Marshall was, as you know, an idealist; so much so that Keynes has said of him that he 'was too anxious to do good'.[4] The last thing I wish to do is to claim him for sociology on that account. It is true that some sociologists have suffered from a similar affliction of benevolence, often to the detriment of their intellectual performance, but I should hate to distinguish the economist from the sociologist by saying that the one should be ruled by his head while the other may be swayed by his heart. For every honest sociologist, like every honest economist, knows that the choice of ends or ideals lies outside the field of social science and within the field of social philosophy. But idealism made Marshall pas-

3

sionately eager to put the science of economics at the service of policy by using it–as a science may legitimately be used–to lay bare the full nature and content of the problems with which policy has to deal and to assess the relative efficacy of alternative means for the achievement of given ends. And he realised that, even in the case of what would naturally be regarded as economic problems, the science of economics was not of itself able fully to render these two services. For they involved the consideration of social forces which are as immune to attack by the economist's tape-measure as was the croquet ball to the blows which Alice tried in vain to strike with the head of her flamingo. It was, perhaps, on this account that, in certain moods, Marshall felt a quite unwarranted disappointment at his achievements, and even expressed regret that he had preferred economics to psychology, a science which might have brought him nearer to the pulse and life-blood of society and given him a deeper understanding of human aspirations.

It would be easy to cite many passages in which Marshall was drawn to speak of these elusive factors of whose importance he was so firmly convinced, but I prefer to confine my attention to one essay whose theme comes very near to that which I have chosen for these lectures. It is a paper he read to the Cambridge Reform Club in 1873 on *The Future of the Working Classes,* and it has been republished in the memorial volume edited by Professor Pigou. There are some textual differences between the two editons which, I understand, are to be attributed to corrections made by Marshall himself after the original version had appeared in print as a pamphlet.[5] I was reminded of this essay by my colleague, Professor Phelps Brown, who made use of it in his inaugural lecture last November.[6] It is equally well suited to my purpose today, because in it Marshall, while examining one facet of the problem of social equality from the point of view of economic cost, came right up to the frontier beyond which lies the territory of sociology, crossed it, and made a brief excursion on the other side. His action could be interpreted as a challenge to sociology to send an emissary to meet him at the frontier, and to join with him in the task of converting no-man's-land into common ground. I have been presumptuous enough to answer the challenge by setting out to travel, as historian and sociologist, towards a point on the economic frontier of that same general theme, the problem of social equality.

In his Cambridge paper Marshall posed the question 'whether there be valid ground for the opinion that the amelioration of the working classes has limits beyond which it cannot pass'. 'The question', he said, 'is not whether all men will ultimately be equal–that they certainly will not–but whether progress may not go on steadily, if slowly, till, by occupation at least, every man is a gentleman. I hold that it may, and that it will.'[7] His faith was based on the belief that the distinguishing feature of the working classes was heavy and excessive labour, and that the volume of such labour could be greatly reduced. Looking round he found evidence that the skilled artisans, whose labour was not deadening and soul-destroying, were already rising towards the condition which he foresaw as the ultimate achievement of all. They are learning, he said, to value education and leisure more than 'mere increase of wages and material comforts'. They are 'steadily developing independence and a manly respect for themselves and, therefore, a courteous respect for others; they are steadily accepting the private and public duties of a citizen; steadily increasing their grasp of the truth that they are men, and not producing machines. They are steadily becoming gentlemen.'[8] When technical advance has reduced heavy labour to a minimum, and that minimum is divided in small amounts among all, then, 'in so far as the working classes are men who have such excessive work to do, in so far will the working classes have been abolished.'[9]

Marshall realised that he might be accused of adopting the ideas of the socialists, whose works, as he has himself told us, he had, during this period of his life, been studying with great hopes and with greater disappointment. For, he said: 'The picture to be drawn will resemble in some respects those which have been shown to us by the Socialists, that noble set of untutored enthusiasts who attributed to all men an unlimited capacity for those self-forgetting virtues that they found in their own breasts.'[10] His reply was that his system differed fundamentally from socialism in that it would preserve the essentials of a free market. He held, however, that the state would have to make some use of its power of compulsion, if his ideals were to be realised. It must compel children to go to school, because the uneducated cannot appreciate, and therefore freely choose, the good things which distinguish the life of gentlemen from that of the working classes. 'It is bound to compel them and to help them to take the first step upwards; and it is bound to help them, if they will, to make many steps upwards.'[11] Notice that only the first step is compulsory. Free choice takes over as soon as the capacity to choose has been created.

Marshall's paper was built round a sociological hypothesis and an economic calculation. The calculation provided the answer to his initial question, by showing that world resources and productivity might be expected to prove sufficient to provide the material bases needed to enable every man to be a gentleman. In other words, the cost of providing education for all and of eliminating heavy and excessive labour could be met. There was no impassable limit to the amelioration

of the working classes–at least on this side of the point that Marshall
described as the goal. In working out these sums Marshall was using the
ordinary techniques of the economist, though admittedly he was applying them to a problem which involved a high degree of speculation.
The sociological hypothesis does not lie so completely on the surface.
A little excavation is needed to uncover its total shape. The essence of it
is contained in the passages I have quoted, but Marshall gives us an
additional clue by suggesting that, when we say a man belongs to the
working classes, 'we are thinking of the effect that his work produces
on him rather than the effect that he produces on his work.'[12] This is
certainly not the sort of definition we should expect from an economist,
and, in fact, it would hardly be fair to treat it as a definition at all or to
subject it to close and critical examination. The phrase was intended to
catch the imagination, and to point to the general direction in which
Marshall's thoughts were moving. And that direction was away from a
quantitative assessment of standards of living in terms of goods con-
sumed and services enjoyed towards a qualitative assessment of life as
a whole in terms of the essential elements in civilisation or culture. He
accepted as right and proper a wide range of quantitative or economic
inequality, but condemned the qualitative inequality or difference between the man who was, 'by occupation at least, a gentleman' and the
man who was not. We can, I think, without doing violence to Marshall's
meaning, replace the word 'gentleman' by the word 'civilised'. For it is
clear that he was taking as the standard of civilised life the conditions
regarded by his generation as appropriate to a gentleman. We can go on
to say that the claim of all to enjoy these conditions is a claim to be
admitted to a share in the social heritage, which in turn means a claim
to be accepted as full members of the society, that is, as citizens.

Such, I think, is the sociological hypothesis latent in Marshall's essay.
It postulates that there is a kind of basic human equality associated with
the concept of full membership of a community–or, as I should say, of
citizenship–which is not inconsistent with the inequalities which distinguish the various economic levels in the society. In other words, the
inequality of the social class system may be acceptable provided the
equality of citizenship is recognised. Marshall did not identify the life of
a gentleman with the status of citizenship. To do so would have been to
express his ideal in terms of legal rights to which all men were entitled.
That, in turn, would have put the responsibility for granting those rights
fair and square on the shoulders of the state, and so led, step by step, to
acts of state interference which he would have deplored. When he
mentioned citizenship as something which skilled artisans learned to
appreciate in the course of developing into gentlemen, he mentioned

only its duties and not its rights. He thought of it as a way of life growing within a man, not presented to him from without. He recognised only one definite right, the right of children to be educated, and in this case alone did he approve the use of compulsory powers by the state to achieve his object. He could hardly go further without imperilling his own criterion for distinguishing his system from socialism in any form—the preservation of the freedom of the competitive market.

Nevertheless, his sociological hypothesis lies as near to the heart of our problem today as it did three-quarters of a century ago–in fact nearer. The basic human equality of membership, at which I maintain that he hinted, has been enriched with new substance and invested with a formidable array of rights. It has developed far beyond what he foresaw, or would have wished. It has been clearly identified with the status of citizenship. And it is time we examined his hypothesis and posed his questions afresh, to see if the answers are still the same. Is it still true that basic equality, when enriched in substance and embodied in the formal rights of citizenship, is consistent with the inequalities of social class? I shall suggest that our society today assumes that the two are still compatible, so much so that citizenship has itself become, in certain respects, the architect of legitimate social inequality. Is it still true that the basic equality can be created and preserved without invading the freedom of the competitive market? Obviously it is not true. Our modern system is frankly a socialist system, not one whose authors are, as Marshall was, eager to distinguish it from socialism. But it is equally obvious that the market still functions–within limits. Here is another possible conflict of principles which demands examination. And thirdly, what is the effect of the marked shift of emphasis from duties to rights? Is this an inevitable feature of modern citizenship–inevitable and irreversible? Finally, I want to put Marshall's initial question again in a new form. He asked if there were limits beyond which the amelioration of the working classes could not pass, and he was thinking of limits set by natural resources and productivity. I shall ask whether there appear to be limits beyond which the modern drive towards social equality cannot, or is unlikely to, pass, and I shall be thinking, not of the economic cost (I leave that vital question to the economists), but of the limits inherent in the principles that inspire the drive. But the modern drive towards social equality is, I believe, the latest phase of an evolution of citizenship which has been in continuous progress for some 250 years. My first task, therefore, must be to prepare the ground for an attack on the problems of today by digging for a while in the subsoil of past history.

2. The Development of Citizenship to the End of the Nineteenth Century

I shall be running true to type as a sociologist if I begin by saying that I propose to divide citizenship into three parts. But the analysis is, in this case, dictated by history even more clearly than by logic. I shall call these three parts, or elements, civil, political and social. The civil element is composed of the rights necessary for individual freedom–liberty of the person, freedom of speech, thought and faith, the right to own property and to conclude valid contracts, and the right to justice. The last is of a different order from the others, because it is the right to defend and assert all one's rights on terms of equality with others and by due process of law. This shows us that the institutions most directly associated with civil rights are the courts of justice. By the political element I mean the right to participate in the exercise of political power, as a member of a body invested with political authority or as an elector of the members of such a body. The corresponding institutions are parliament and councils of local government. By the social element I mean the whole range from the right to a modicum of economic welfare and security to the right to share to the full in the social heritage and to live the life of a civilised being according to the standards prevailing in the society. The institutions most closely connected with it are the educational system and the social services.[13]

In early times these three strands were wound into a single thread. The rights were blended because the institutions were amalgamated. As Maitland said: 'The further back we trace our history the more impossible it is for us to draw strict lines of demarcation between the various functions of the State: the same institution is a legislative assembly, a governmental council and a court of law.... Everywhere, as we pass from the ancient to the modern, we see what the fashionable philosophy calls differentiation.'[14] Maitland is speaking here of the fusion of political and civil institutions and rights. But a man's social rights, too, were part of the same amalgam, and derived from the status which also determined the kind of justice he could get and where he could get it, and the way in which he could take part in the administration of the affairs of the community of which he was a member. But this status was not one of citizenship in our modern sense. In feudal society status was the hallmark of class and the measure of inequality. There was no uniform collection of rights and duties with which all men–noble and common, free and serf–were endowed by virtue of their membership of the society. There was, in this sense, no principle of the equality of citizens to set against the principle of the inequality of classes. In the medieval towns, on the other hand, examples of genuine and equal citizenship can be found. But its specific rights and duties were strictly local, whereas the citizenship whose history I wish to trace is, by definition, national. Its evolution involved a double process, of fusion and of separation. The fusion was geographical, the separation functional. The first important step dates from the twelfth century, when royal justice was established with effective power to define and defend the civil rights of the individual–such as they then were–on the basis, not of local custom, but of the common law of the land. As institutions the courts were national, but specialised. Parliament followed, concentrating in itself the political powers of national government and shedding all but a small residue of the judicial functions which formerly belonged to the Curia Regis, that 'sort of constitutional protoplasm out of which will in time be evolved the various councils of the crown, the houses of parliament, and the courts of law'.[15] Finally, the social rights which had been rooted in membership of the village community, the town and the guild, were gradually dissolved by economic change until nothing remained but the Poor Law, again a specialised institution which acquired a national foundation, although it continued to be locally administered.

Two important consequences followed. First, when the institutions on which the three elements of citizenship depended parted company, it became possible for each to go its separate way, travelling at its own speed under the direction of its own peculiar principles. Before long they were spread far out along the course, and it is only in the present century, in fact I might say only within the last few months, that the three runners have come abreast of one another.

Secondly, institutions that were national and specialised could not belong so intimately to the life of the social groups they served as those that were local and of a general character. The remoteness of parliament was due to the mere size of its constituency; the remoteness of the courts, to the technicalities of their law and their procedure, which made it necessary for the citizen to employ legal experts to advise him as to the nature of his rights and to help him to obtain them. It has been pointed out again and again that, in the Middle Ages, participation in public affairs was more a duty than a right. Men owed suit and service to the court appropriate to their class and neighbourhood. The court belonged to them and they to it, and they had access to it because it needed them and because they had knowledge of its affairs. But the result of the twin process of fusion and separation was that the machinery giving access to the institutions on which the rights of citizenship depended had to be shaped afresh. In the case of political rights the story is the familiar one of the franchise and the qualifications for membership of parliament. In the case of civil rights the issue hangs on the jurisdiction of the various courts, the privileges of the legal profession, and above all on the liability to meet the costs of litigation. In the case of social rights the centre of the stage is occupied by the Law of Settlement and Removal and the various forms of means test. All this apparatus combined to decide, not merely what rights were recognised in principle, but also to what extent rights recognised in principle could be enjoyed in practice.

When the three elements of citizenship parted company, they were soon barely on speaking terms. So complete was the divorce between them that it is possible, without doing too much violence to historical accuracy, to assign the formative period in the life of each to a different century–civil rights to the eighteenth, political to the nineteenth and social to the twentieth. These periods must, of course, be treated with reasonable elasticity, and there is some evident overlap, especially between the last two.

To make the eighteenth century cover the formative period of civil rights it must be stretched backwards to include Habeas Corpus, the Toleration Act, and the abolition of the censorship of the press; and it must be extended forwards to include Catholic Emancipation, the repeal of the Combination Acts, and the successful end of the battle for the freedom of the press associated with the names of Cobbett and Richard Carlile. It could then be more accurately, but less briefly, described as the period between the Revolution and the first Reform Act. By the end of that period, when political rights made their first infantile attempt to walk in 1832, civil rights had come to man's estate and bore, in most essentials, the appearance that they have today.[16] 'The specific work of the earlier Hanoverian epoch', writes Trevelyan, 'was the establishment of the rule of law; and that law, with all its grave faults, was at least a law of freedom. On that solid foundation all our subsequent reforms were built.'[17] This eighteenth-century achievement, interrupted by the French Revolution and completed after it, was in large measure the work of the courts, both in their daily practice and also in a series of famous cases in some of which they were fighting against parliament in defence of individual liberty. The most celebrated actor in this drama was, I suppose, John Wilkes, and, although we may deplore the absence in him of those noble and saintly qualities which we should like to find in our national heroes, we cannot complain if the cause of liberty is sometimes championed by a libertine.

In the economic field the basic civil right is the right to work, that is to say the right to follow the occupation of one's choice in the place of one's choice, subject only to legitimate demands for preliminary technical training. This right had been denied by both statute and custom; on the one hand by the Elizabethan Statute of Artificers, which confined certain occupations to certain social classes, and on the other by local regulations reserving employment in a town to its own members and by the use of apprenticeship as an instrument of exclusion rather than of recruitment. The recognition of the right involved the formal acceptance of a fundamental change of attitude. The old assumption that local and group monopolies were in the public interest, because 'trade and traffic cannot be maintained or increased without order and government',[18] was replaced by the new assumption that such restrictions were an offence against the liberty of the subject and a menace to the prosperity of the nation. As in the case of the other civil rights, the courts of law played a decisive part in promoting and registering the advance of the new principle. The Common Law was elastic enough for the judges to apply it in a manner which, almost imperceptibly, took account of gradual changes in circumstances and opinion and eventually installed the heresy of the past as the orthodoxy of the present. The Common Law is largely a matter of common sense, as witness the judgement given by Chief Justice Holt in the case of Mayor of Winton *v.* Wilks (1705): 'All people are at liberty to live in Winchester, and how can they be restrained from using the lawful means of living there? Such a custom is an injury to the party and a prejudice to the public.'[19] Custom was one of the two great obstacles to the change. But, when ancient custom in the technical sense was clearly at variance with contemporary custom in the sense of the generally accepted way of life, its defences began to crumble fairly rapidly before the attacks of a Common Law which had, as early as 1614, expressed its abhorrence of 'all monopolies which prohibit any from working in any lawful trade'.[20] The other obstacle was statute law, and the judges struck some shrewd blows even against this doughty opponent. In 1756 Lord Mansfield described the Elizabethan Statute of Artificers as a penal law, in restraint of natural right and contrary to the Common Law of the kingdom. He added that 'the policy upon which the Act was made is, from experience, become doubtful'.[21]

By the beginning of the nineteenth century this principle of individual economic freedom was accepted as axiomatic. You are probably familiar with the passage quoted by the Webbs from the report of the Select Committee of 1811, which states that:

no interference of the legislature with the freedom of trade, or with the perfect liberty of every individual to dispose of his time and of his labour in the way and on the terms which he may judge most conducive to his own interest, can take place without violating general principles of the first importance to the prosperity and happiness of the community.[22]

The repeal of the Elizabethan statutes followed quickly, as the belated recognition of a revolution which had already taken place.

The story of civil rights in their formative period is one of the gradual addition of new rights to a status that already existed and was held to appertain to all adult members of the community–or perhaps one should say to all male members, since the status of women, or at least of married women, was in some important respects peculiar. This democratic, or universal, character of the status arose naturally from the fact that it was essentially the status of freedom, and in seventeenth-century England all men were free. Servile status, or villeinage by blood, had lingered on as a patent anachronism in the days of Elizabeth, but vanished soon afterwards. This change from servile to free labour has been described by Professor Tawney as 'a high landmark in the development both of economic and political society', and as 'the final triumph of the common law' in regions from which it had been excluded for four centuries. Henceforth the English peasant 'is a member of a society in which there is, nominally at least, one law for all men'.[23] The liberty which his predecessors had won by fleeing into the free towns had become his by right. In the towns the terms 'freedom' and 'citizenship' were inter-changeable. When freedom became universal, citizenship grew from a local into a national institution.

The story of political rights is different both in time and in character. The formative period began, as I have said, in the early nineteenth century, when the civil rights attached to the status of freedom had already acquired sufficient substance to justify us in speaking of a general status of citizenship. And, when it began, it consisted, not in the creation of new rights to enrich a status already enjoyed by all, but in the granting of old rights to new sections of the population. In the eighteenth century political rights were defective, not in content, but in distribution–defec-tive, that is to say, by the standards of democratic citizenship. The Act of 1832 did little, in a purely quantitative sense, to remedy that defect. After it was passed the voters still amounted to less than one-fifth of the adult male population. The franchise was still a group monopoly, but it had taken the first step towards becoming a monopoly of a kind acceptable to the ideas of nineteenth-century capitalism–a monopoly which could, with some degree of plausibility, be described as open and not closed. A closed group monopoly is one into which no man can force his way by his own efforts; admission is at the pleasure of the existing members of the group. The description fits a considerable part of the borough franchise before 1832; and it is not too wide of the mark when applied to the franchise based on freehold ownership of land. Freeholds are not always to be had for the asking, even if one has the money to buy them, especially in an age in which families look on their lands as the social, as well as the economic, foundation of their existence. Therefore the Act of 1832, by abolishing rotten boroughs and by extending the franchise to leaseholders and occupying tenants of sufficient economic substance, opened the monopoly by recognising the political claims of those who could produce the normal evidence of success in the economic struggle.

It is clear that, if we maintain that in the nineteenth century citizenship in the form of civil rights was universal, the political franchise was not one of the rights of citizenship. It was the privilege of a limited economic class, whose limits were extended by each successive Reform Act. It can nevertheless be argued that citizenship in this period was not politically meaningless. It did not confer a right, but it recognised a capacity. No sane and law-abiding citizen was debarred by personal status from acquiring and recording a vote. He was free to earn, to save, to buy property or to rent a house, and to enjoy whatever political rights were attached to these economic achievements. His civil rights entitled him, and electoral reform increasingly enabled him, to do this.

It was, as we shall see, appropriate that nineteenth-century capitalist society should treat political rights as a secondary product of civil rights. It was equally appropriate that the twentieth century should abandon this position and attach political rights directly and independently to citizenship as such. This vital change of principle was put into effect when the Act of 1918, by adopting manhood suffrage, shifted the basis of political rights from economic substance to personal status. I say 'manhood' deliberately in order to emphasise the great significance of this reform quite apart from the second, and no less important, reform introduced at the same time–namely the enfranchisement of women. But the Act of 1918 did not fully establish the political equality of all in terms of the rights of citizenship. Remnants of an inequality based on differences of economic substance lingered on until, only last year, plural voting (which had already been reduced to dual voting) was finally abolished.

When I assigned the formative periods of the three elements of citizenship each to a separate century–civil rights to the eighteenth, political to the nineteenth and social to the twentieth–I said that there was a considerable overlap between the last two. I propose to confine what I have to say now about social rights to this overlap, in order that I may complete my historical survey to the end of the nineteenth century, and draw my conclusions from it, before turning my attention to the second half of my subject, a study of our present experiences and their immediate antecedents. In this second act of the drama social rights will occupy the centre of the stage.

The original source of social rights was membership of local communities and functional associations. This source was supplemented and progressively replaced by a Poor Law and a system of wage regulation which were nationally conceived and locally administered. The latter–the system of wage regulation–was rapidly decaying in the eighteenth century, not only because industrial change made it administratively impossible, but also because it was incompatible with the new conception of civil rights in the economic sphere, with its emphasis on the right to work where and at what you pleased under a contract of your own making. Wage regulation infringed this individualist principle of the free contract of employment.

The Poor Law was in a somewhat ambiguous position. Elizabethan legislation had made of it something more than a means for relieving destitution and suppressing vagrancy, and its constructive aims suggested an interpretation of social welfare reminiscent of the more primitive, but more genuine, social rights which it had largely superseded. The Elizabethan Poor Law was, after all, one item in a broad programme of economic planning whose general object was, not to create a new social order, but to preserve the existing one with the minimum of essential change. As the pattern of the old order dissolved under the blows of a competitive economy, and the plan disintegrated, the Poor Law was left high and dry as an isolated survival from which the idea of social rights was gradually drained away. But at the very end of the eighteenth century there occurred a final struggle between the old and the new, between the planned (or patterned) society and the competitive economy. And in this battle citizenship was divided against itself; social rights sided with the old and civil with the new.

In his book *Origins of our Time*, Karl Polanyi attributes to the Speenhamland system of poor relief an importance which some readers may find surprising. To him it seems to mark and symbolise the end of an epoch. Through it the old order rallied its retreating forces and delivered a spirited attack into the enemy's country. That, at least, is how I should describe its significance in the history of citizenship. The Speenhamland system offered, in effect, a guaranteed minimum wage and family allowances, combined with the right to work or maintenance. That, even by modern standards, is a substantial body of social rights, going far beyond what one might regard as the proper province of the Poor Law. And it was fully realised by the originators of the scheme that the Poor Law was being invoked to do what wage regulation was no longer able to accomplish. For the Poor Law was the last remains of a system which tried to adjust real income to the social needs and status of the citizen and not solely to the market value of his labour. But this attempt to inject an element of social security into the very structure of the wage system through the instrumentality of the Poor Law was doomed to failure, not only because of its disastrous practical consequences, but also because it was utterly obnoxious to the prevailing spirit of the times.

In this brief episode of our history we see the Poor Law as the aggressive champion of the social rights of citizenship. In the succeeding phase we find the attacker driven back far behind his original position. By the Act of 1834 the Poor Law renounced all claim to trespass on the territory of the wages system, or to interfere with the forces of the free market. It offered relief only to those who, through age or sickness, were incapable of continuing the battle, and to those other weaklings who gave up the struggle, admitted defeat, and cried for mercy. The tentative move towards the concept of social security was reversed. But more than that, the minimal social rights that remained were detached from the status of citizenship. The Poor Law treated the claims of the poor, not as an integral part of the rights of the citizen, but as an alternative to them–as claims which could be met only if the claimants ceased to be citizens in any true sense of the word. For paupers forfeited in practice the civil right of personal liberty, by internment in the workhouse, and they forfeited by law any political rights they might possess. This disability of disfranchisement remained in being until 1918, and the significance of its final removal has, perhaps, not been fully appreciated. The stigma which clung to poor relief expressed the deep feelings of a people who understood that those who accepted relief must cross the road that separated the community of citizens from the outcast company of the destitute.

The Poor Law is not an isolated example of this divorce of social rights from the status of citizenship. The early Factory Acts show the same tendency. Although in fact they led to an improvement of working conditions and a reduction of working hours to the benefit of all employed in the industries to which they applied, they meticulously refrained from giving this protection directly to the adult male–the citizen *par excellence*. And they did so out of respect for his status as a citizen, on the grounds that enforced protective measures curtailed the civil right to conclude a free contract of employment. Protection was confined to women and children, and champions of women's rights were quick to detect the implied insult. Women were protected because they were not citizens. If they wished to enjoy full and responsible citizenship, they must forgo protection. By the end of the nineteenth century such arguments had become obsolete, and the factory code had become one of the pillars in the edifice of social rights.

The history of education shows superficial resemblances to that of factory legislation. In both cases the nineteenth century was, for the most part, a period in which the foundations of social rights were laid, but the principle of social rights as an integral part of the status of citizenship was either expressly denied or not definitely admitted. But there are significant differences. Education, as Marshall recognised when he singled it out as a fit object of state action, is a service of a unique kind. It is easy to say that the recognition of the right of children to be educated does not affect the status of citizenship any more than does the recognition of the right of children to be protected from overwork and dangerous machinery, simply because children, by definition, cannot be citizens. But such a statement is misleading. The education of children has a direct bearing on citizenship, and, when the state guarantees that all children shall be educated, it has the requirements and the nature of citizenship definitely in mind. It is trying to stimulate the growth of citizens in the making. The right to education is a genuine social right of citizenship, because the aim of education during childhood is to shape the future adult. Fundamentally it should be regarded, not as the right of the child to go to school, but as the right of the adult citizen to have been educated. And there is here no conflict with civil rights as interpreted in an age of individualism. For civil rights are designed for use by reasonable and intelligent persons, who have learned to read and write. Education is a necessary prerequisite of civil freedom.

But, by the end of the nineteenth century, elementary education was not only free, it was compulsory. This signal departure from *laissez faire* could, of course, be justified on the grounds that free choice is a right only for mature minds, that children are naturally subject to discipline, and that parents cannot be trusted to do what is in the best interests of their children. But the principle goes deeper than that. We have here a personal right combined with a public duty to exercise the right. Is the public duty imposed merely for the benefit of the individual–because children cannot fully appreciate their own interests and parents may be unfit to enlighten them? I hardly think that this can be an adequate explanation. It was increasingly recognised, as the nineteenth century wore on, that political democracy needed an educated electorate, and that scientific manufacture needed educated workers and technicians. The duty to improve and civilise oneself is therefore a social duty, and not merely a personal one, because the social health of a society depends upon the civilisation of its members. And a community that enforces this duty has begun to realise that its culture is an organic unity and its civilisation a national heritage. It follows that the growth of public elementary education during the nineteenth century was the first decisive step on the road to the re-establishment of the social rights of citizenship in the twentieth.

When Marshall read his paper to the Cambridge Reform Club, the state was just preparing to shoulder the responsibility he attributed to it when he said that it was 'bound to compel them [the children] and help them to take the first step upwards'. But this would not go far towards realising his ideal of making every man a gentleman, nor was that in the least the intention. And as yet there was little sign of any desire 'to help them, if they will, to make many steps upwards'. The idea was in the air, but it was not a cardinal point of policy. In the early nineties the London County Council, through its Technical Education Board, instituted a scholarship system which Beatrice Webb obviously regarded as epoch-making. For she wrote of it:

> In its popular aspect this was an educational ladder of unprecedented dimensions. It was, indeed, among educational ladders the most gigantic in extent, the most elaborate in its organization of 'intakes' and promotions, and the most diversified in kinds of excellence selected and in types of training provided that existed anywhere in the world.[24]

The enthusiasm of these words enables us to see how far we have advanced our standards since those days.

3. The Early Impact of Citizenship on Social Class

So far my aim has been to trace in outline the development of citizenship in England to the end of the nineteenth century. For this purpose I have divided citizenship into three elements, civil, political and social. I have tried to show that civil rights came first, and were established in something like their modern form before the first Reform Act was passed in 1832. Political rights came next, and their extension was one of the main features of the nineteenth century, although the principle of universal political citizenship was not recognised until 1918. Social rights, on the other hand, sank to vanishing point in the eighteenth and early nineteenth centuries. Their revival began with the development of public elementary education, but it was not until the twentieth century that they attained to equal partnership with the other two elements in citizenship.

I have as yet said nothing about social class, and I should explain here that social class occupies a secondary position in my theme. I do not propose to embark on the long and difficult task of examining its nature and analysing its components. Time would not allow me to do justice to so formidable a subject. My primary concern is with citizenship, and my special interest is in its impact on social inequality. I shall discuss the nature of social class only so far as is necessary for the pursuit of this special interest. I have paused in the narrative at the end of the nineteenth century because I believe that the impact of citizenship on social inequality after that date was fundamentally different from what it had been before it. That statement is not likely to be disputed. It is the exact nature of the difference that is worth exploring. Before going any further, therefore, I shall try to draw some general conclusions about the impact of citizenship on social inequality in the earlier of the two periods.

Citizenship is a status bestowed on those who are full members of a community. All who possess the status are equal with respect to the rights and duties with which the status is endowed. There is no universal principle that determines what those rights and duties shall be, but societies in which citizenship is a developing institution create an image of an ideal citizenship against which achievement can be measured and towards which aspiration can be directed. The urge forward along the path thus plotted is an urge towards a fuller measure of equality, an enrichment of the stuff of which the status is made and an increase in the number of those on whom the status is bestowed. Social class, on the other hand, is a system of inequality. And it too, like citizenship, can be based on a set of ideals, beliefs and values. It is therefore reasonable to expect that the impact of citizenship on social class should take the form of a conflict between opposing principles. If I am right in my contention that citizenship has been a developing institution in England at least since the latter part of the seventeenth century, then it is clear that its growth coincides with the rise of capitalism, which is a system, not of equality, but of inequality. Here is something that needs explaining. How is it that these two opposing principles could grow and flourish side by side in the same soil? What made it possible for them to be reconciled with one another and to become, for a time at least, allies instead of antagonists? The question is a pertinent one, for it is clear that, in the twentieth century, citizenship and the capitalist class system have been at war.

It is at this point that a closer scrutiny of social class becomes necessary. I cannot attempt to examine all its many and varied forms, but there is one broad distinction between two different types of class which is particularly relevant to my argument. In the first of these class is based on a hierarchy of status, and the difference between one class and another is expressed in terms of legal rights and of established customs which have the essential binding character of law. In its extreme form such a system divides a society into a number of distinct, hereditary human species—patricians, plebeians, serfs, slaves and so forth. Class is, as it were, an institution in its own right, and the whole structure has the quality of a plan, in the sense that it is endowed with meaning and purpose and accepted as a natural order. The civilisation at each level is an expression of this meaning and of this natural order, and differences between social levels are not differences in standard of living, because there is no common standard by which they can be measured. Nor are there any rights–at least none of any significance–which all share in common.[25] The impact of citizenship on such a system was bound to be profoundly disturbing, and even destructive. The rights with which the general status of citizenship was invested were extracted from the hierarchical status system of social class, robbing it of its essential substance. The equality implicit in the concept of citizenship, even though limited in content, undermined the inequality of the class system, which was in principle a total inequality. National justice and a law common to all must inevitably weaken and eventually destroy class justice, and personal freedom, as a universal birthright, must drive out serfdom. No subtle argument is needed to show that citizenship is incompatible with medieval feudalism.

Social class of the second type is not so much an institution in its own right as a by-product of other institutions. Although we may still refer to 'social status', we are stretching the term beyond its strict technical meaning when we do so. Class differences are not established and defined by the laws and customs of the society (in the medieval sense of that phrase), but emerge from the interplay of a variety of factors related to the institutions of property and education and the structure of the national economy. Class cultures dwindle to a minimum, so that it becomes possible, though admittedly not wholly satisfactory, to measure the different levels of economic welfare by reference to a common standard of living. The working classes, instead of inheriting a distinctive though simple culture, are provided with a cheap and shoddy imitation of a civilisation that has become national.

It is true that class still functions. Social inequality is regarded as necessary and purposeful. It provides the incentive to effort and designs the distribution of power. But there is no overall pattern of inequality, in which an appropriate value is attached, a priori, to each social level. Inequality therefore, though necessary, may become excessive. As Patrick Colquhoun said, in a much-quoted passage: 'Without a large proportion of poverty there could be no riches, since riches are the offspring of labour, while labour can result only from a state of poverty... Poverty therefore is a most necessary and indispensable 'ingredient in society, without which nations and communities could not exist in a state of civilisation.'[26] But Colquhoun, while accepting poverty, deplored 'indigence', or, as we should say, destitution. By 'poverty' he meant the situation of a man who, owing to lack of any economic reserves, is obliged to work, and to work hard, in order to live. By 'indigence' he meant the situation of a family which lacks the minimum necessary for decent living. The system of inequality which allowed the former to exist as a driving force inevitably produced a certain amount of the latter as well. Colquhoun, and other humanitarians, regretted this and sought means to alleviate the suffering it caused. But they did not question the justice of the system of inequality as a whole. It could be argued, in defence of its justice, that, although poverty might be necessary, it was not necessary that any particular family should remain poor, or quite as poor as it was. The more you look on wealth as conclusive proof of merit, the more you incline to regard poverty as evidence of failure–but the penalty for failure may seem to be greater than the offence warrants. In such circumstances it is natural that the more unpleasant features of inequality should be treated, rather irresponsibly, as a nuisance, like the black smoke that used to pour unchecked from our factory chimneys. And so in time, as the social conscience stirs to life, class-abatement, like smoke-abatement, becomes a desirable aim to be pursued as far as is compatible with the continued efficiency of the social machine.

But class-abatement in this form was not an attack on the class system. On the contrary it aimed, often quite consciously, at making the class system less vulnerable to attack by alleviating its less defensible consequences. It raised the floor-level in the basement of the social edifice, and perhaps made it rather more hygienic than it was before. But it remained a basement, and the upper stories of the building were unaffected. And the benefits received by the unfortunate did not flow from an enrichment of the status of citizenship. Where they were given officially by the state, this was done by measures which, as I have said, offered alternatives to the rights of citizenship, rather than additions to them. But the major part of the task was left to private charity, and it was the general, though not universal, view of charitable bodies that those who received their help had no personal right to claim it.

Nevertheless it is true that citizenship, even in its early forms, was a principle of equality, and that during this period it was a developing institution. Starting at the point where all men were free and, in theory, capable of enjoying rights, it grew by enriching the body of rights which they were capable of enjoying. But these rights did not conflict with the inequalities of capitalist society; they were, on the contrary, necessary to the maintenance of that particular form of inequality. The explanation lies in the fact that the core of citizenship at this stage was composed of civil rights. And civil rights were indispensable to a competitive market economy. They gave to each man, as part of his individual status, the power to engage as an independent unit in the economic struggle and made it possible to deny to him social protection on the ground that he was equipped with the means to protect himself. Maine's famous dictum that 'the movement of the progressive societies has hitherto been a movement from Status to Contract'[27] expresses a profound truth which has been elaborated, with varying terminology, by many sociologists, but it requires qualification. For both status and contract are present in all but the most primitive societies. Maine himself admitted this when, later in the same book, he wrote that the earliest feudal communities, as contrasted with their archaic predecessors, 'were neither bound together by mere sentiment nor recruited by a fiction. The tie which united them was Contract.'[28] But the contractual element in feudalism coexisted with a class system based on status and, as contract hardened into custom, it helped to perpetuate class status. Custom retained the form of mutual undertakings, but not the reality of a free agreement. Modern contract did not grow out of feudal contract; it marks a new development to whose progress feudalism was an obstacle that had to be swept aside. For modern contract is essentially an agreement between men who are free and equal in status, though not necessarily in power. Status was not eliminated from the social system. Differential status, associated with class, function and family, was replaced by the single uniform status of citizenship, which provided the foundation of equality on which the structure of inequality could be built.

When Maine wrote, this status was clearly an aid, and not a menace, to capitalism and the free-market economy, because it was dominated by civil rights, which confer the legal capacity to strive for the things one would like to possess but do not guarantee the possession of any of them. A property right is not a right to possess property, but a right to acquire it, if you can, and to protect it, if you can get it. But, if you use these arguments to explain to a pauper that his property rights are the same as those of a millionaire, he will probably accuse you of quibbling. Similarly, the right to freedom of speech has little real substance if, from lack of education, you have nothing to say that is worth saying, and no means of making yourself heard if you say it. But these blatant inequalities are not due to defects in civil rights, but to lack of social rights, and social rights in the mid-nineteenth century were in the doldrums. The Poor Law was an aid, not a menace, to capitalism, because it relieved industry of all social responsibility outside the contract of employment, while sharpening the edge of competition in the labour market. Elementary schooling was also an aid, because it increased the value of the worker without educating him above his station.

But it would be absurd to contend that the civil rights enjoyed in the eighteenth and nineteenth centuries were free from defects, or that they were as egalitarian in practice as they professed to be in principle. Equality before the law did not exist. The right was there, but the remedy might frequently prove to be out of reach. The barriers between rights and remedies were of two kinds: the first arose from class prejudice and partiality, the second from the automatic effects of the unequal distribution of wealth, working through the price system. Class prejudice, which undoubtedly coloured the whole administration of justice in the eighteenth century, cannot be eliminated by law, but only by social education and the building of a tradition of impartiality. This is a slow and difficult process, which presupposes a change in the climate of thought throughout the upper ranks of society. But it is a process which I think it is fair to say has been successfully accomplished, in the sense that the tradition of impartiality as between social classes is firmly established in our civil justice. And it is interesting that this should have happened without any fundamental change in the class structure of the legal profession. We have no exact knowledge on this point, but I doubt whether the picture has radically altered since Professor Ginsberg found that the proportion of those admitted to Lincoln's Inn whose fathers were wage-earners had risen from 0.4 per cent in 1904–8 to 1.8 per cent in 1923–7, and that at this latter date nearly 72 per cent were sons of professional men, high-ranking business men and gentlemen.[29] The decline of class prejudice as a barrier to the full enjoyment of rights is, therefore, due less to the dilution of class monopoly in the legal profession than to the spread in all classes of a more humane and realistic sense of social equality.

It is interesting to compare with this the corresponding development in the field of political rights. Here too class prejudice, expressed through the intimidation of the lower classes by the upper, prevented the free exercise of the right to vote by the newly enfranchised. In this case a practical remedy was available, in the secret ballot. But that was not enough. Social education, and a change of mental climate, were needed as well. And, even when voters felt free from undue influence, it still took some time to break down the idea, prevalent in the working as well as other classes, that the representatives of the people, and still more the members of the government, should be drawn from among the élites who were born, bred and educated for leadership. Class monopoly in politics, unlike class monopoly in law, has definitely been overthrown. Thus, in these two fields, the same goal has been reached by rather different paths.

The removal of the second obstacle, the effects of the unequal distribution of wealth, was technically a simple matter in the case of political rights, because it costs little or nothing to register a vote.

Nevertheless, wealth can be used to influence an election, and a series of measures was adopted to reduce this influence. The earlier ones, which go back to the seventeenth century, were directed against bribery and corruption, but the later ones, especially from 1883 onwards, had the wider aim of limiting election expenses in general, in order that candidates of unequal wealth might fight on more or less equal terms. The need for such equalising measures has now greatly diminished, since working-class candidates can get financial support from party and other funds. Restrictions which prevent competitive extravagance are, therefore, probably welcomed by all. It remained to open the House of Commons to men of all classes, regardless of wealth, first by abolishing the property qualification for members, and then by introducing payment of members in 1911.

It has proved far more difficult to achieve similar results in the field of civil rights, because litigation, unlike voting, is very expensive. Court fees are not high, but counsel's fees and solicitor's charges may mount up to very large sums indeed. Since a legal action takes the form of a contest, each party feels that his chances of winning will be improved if he secures the services of better champions than those employed on the other side. There is, of course, some truth in this, but not as much as is popularly believed. But the effect in litigation, as in elections, is to introduce an element of competitive extravagance which makes it difficult to estimate in advance what the costs of an action will amount to. In addition, our system by which costs are normally awarded to the winner increases the risk and the uncertainty. A man of limited means, knowing that, if he loses, he will have to pay his opponent's costs (after they have been pruned by the Taxing Master) as well as his own, may easily be frightened into accepting an unsatisfactory settlement, especially if his opponent is wealthy enough not to be bothered by any such considerations. And even if he wins, the taxed costs he recovers will usually be less than his actual expenditure, and often considerably less. So that, if he has been induced to fight his case expensively, the victory may not be worth the price paid.

What, then, has been done to remove these barriers to the full and equal exercise of civil rights? Only one thing of real substance, the establishment in 1846 of the County Courts to provide cheap justice for the common people. This important innovation has had a profound and beneficial effect on our legal system, and done much to develop a proper sense of the importance of the case brought by the small man—which is often a very big case by his standards. But County Court costs are not negligible, and the jurisdiction of the County Courts is limited. The second major step taken was the development of a poor person's procedure, under which a small fraction of the poorer members of the community could sue *in forma pauperis*, practically free of all cost, being assisted by the gratuitous and voluntary services of the legal profession. But, as the income limit was extremely low (£2 a week since 1919), and the procedure did not apply in the County Courts, it has had little effect except in matrimonial causes. The supplementary service of free legal advice was, until recently, provided by the unaided efforts of voluntary bodies. But the problem has not been overlooked, nor the reality of the defects in our system denied. It has attracted increasing attention during the last hundred years. The machinery of the Royal Commission and the Committee has been used repeatedly, and some reforms of procedure have resulted. Two such Committees are at work now, but it would be most improper for me to make any reference to their deliberations.[30] A third, which started earlier, issued a report on which is based the Legal Aid and Advice Bill laid before parliament just three months ago.[31] This is a bold measure, going far beyond anything previously attempted for the assistance of the poorer litigants, and I shall have more to say about it later on.

It is apparent from the events I have briefly narrated that there developed, in the latter part of the nineteenth century, a growing interest in equality as a principle of social justice and an appreciation of the fact that the formal recognition of an equal capacity for rights was not enough. In theory even the complete removal of all the barriers that separated civil rights from their remedies would not have interfered with the principles or the class structure of the capitalist system. It would, in fact, have created a situation which many supporters of the competitive market economy falsely assumed to be already in existence. But in practice the attitude of mind which inspired the efforts to remove these barriers grew out of a conception of equality which overstepped these narrow limits, the conception of equal social worth, not merely of equal natural rights. Thus although citizenship, even by the end of the nineteenth century, had done little to reduce social inequality, it had helped to guide progress into the path which led directly to the egalitarian policies of the twentieth century.

It also had an integrating effect, or, at least, was an important ingredient in a integrating process. In a passage I quoted just now Maine spoke of pre-feudal societies as bound together by a sentiment and recruited by a fiction. He was referring to kinship, or the fiction of common descent. Citizenship requires a bond of a different kind, a direct sense of community membership based on loyalty to a civilisation which is a common possession. It is a loyalty of free men endowed with rights and protected by a common law. Its growth is stimulated both by the struggle to win those rights and by their enjoyment when won. We see this clearly in the eighteenth century, which saw the birth, not only of modern civil rights, but also of modern national consciousness. The familiar instruments of modern democracy were fashioned by the upper classes and then handed down, step by step, to the lower: political journalism for the intelligentsia was followed by newspapers for all who could read, public meetings, propaganda campaigns and associations for the furtherance of public causes. Repressive measures and taxes were quite unable to stop the flood. And with it came a patriotic nationalism, expressing the unity underlying these controversial outbursts. How deep or widespread this was it is difficult to say, but there can be no doubt about the vigour of its outward manifestation. We still use those typically eighteenth-century songs, 'God Save the King' and 'Rule Britannia', but we omit the passages which would offend our modern, and more modest, sensibilities. This jingo patriotism, and the 'popular and parliamentary agitation' which Temperley found to be 'the main factor in causing the war' of Jenkin's ear,[32] were new phenomena in which can be recognised the first small trickle which grew into the broad stream of the national war efforts of the twentieth century.

This growing national consciousness, this awakening public opinion, and these first stirrings of a sense of community membership and common heritage did not have any material effect on class structure and social inequality for the simple and obvious reason that, even at the end of the nineteenth century, the mass of the working people did not wield effective political power. By that time the franchise was fairly wide, but those who had recently received the vote had not yet learned how to use it. The political rights of citizenship, unlike the civil rights, were full of potential danger to the capitalist system, although those who were cautiously extending them down the social scale probably did not realise quite how great the danger was. They could hardly be expected to foresee what vast changes could be brought about by the peaceful use of political power, without a violent and bloody revolution. The planned society and the welfare state had not yet risen over the horizon or come within the view of the practical politician. The foundations of the market economy and the contractual system seemed strong enough to stand against any probable assault. In fact, there were some grounds for expecting that the working classes, as they became educated, would accept the basic principles of the system and be content to rely for their protection and progress on the civil rights of citizenship, which contained no obvious menace to competitive capitalism. Such a view was encouraged by the fact that one of the main achievements of political power in the later nineteenth century was the recognition of the right of collective bargaining. This meant that social progress was being sought by strengthening civil rights, not by creating social rights; through the use of contract in the open market, not through a minimum wage and social security. But this interpretation underrates the significance of this extension of civil rights in the economic sphere. For civil rights were in origin intensely individual, and that is why they harmonised with the individualistic phase of capitalism. By the device of incorporation groups were enabled to act legally as individuals. This important development did not go unchallenged, and limited liability was widely denounced as an infringement of individual responsibility. But the position of trade unions was even more anomalous, because they did not seek or obtain incorporation. They can, therefore, exercise vital civil rights collectively on behalf of their members without formal collective responsibility, while the individual responsibility of the workers in relation to contract is largely unenforceable. These civil rights became, for the workers, an instrument for raising their social and economic status, that is to say, for establishing the claim that they, as citizens, were entitled to certain social rights. But the normal method of establishing social rights is by the exercise of political power, for social rights imply an absolute right to a certain standard of civilisation which is conditional only on the discharge of the general duties of citizenship. Their content does not depend on the economic value of the individual claimant. There is therefore a significant difference between a genuine collective bargain through which economic forces in a free market seek to achieve equilibrium and the use of collective civil rights to assert basic claims to the elements of social justice. Thus the acceptance of collective bargaining was not simply a natural extension of civil rights; it represented the transfer of an important process from the political to the civil sphere of citizenship. But 'transfer' is, perhaps, a misleading term, for at the time when this happened the workers either did not posses, or had not yet learned to use, the political right of the franchise. Since then they have obtained and made full use of that right. Trade unionism has, therefore, created a secondary system of industrial citizenship parallel with and supplementary to the system of political citizenship.

It is interesting to compare this development with the history of parliamentary representation. In the early parliaments, says Pollard, 'representation was nowise regarded as a means of expressing individual right or forwarding individual interests. It was communities, not individuals, who were represented.'[33] And, looking at the position on the eve of the Reform Act of 1918, he added: 'Parliament, instead of representing communities or families, is coming to represent nothing but individuals.'³⁴ A system of manhood and womanhood suffrage treats the vote as the voice of the individual. Political parties organise these voices for group action, but they do so nationally and not on the basis of function, locality or interest. In the case of civil rights the movement has been in the opposite direction, not from the representation of communities to that of individuals, but from the representation of individuals to that of communities. And Pollard makes another point. It was a characteristic of the early parliamentary system, he says, that the representatives were those who had the time, the means and the inclination to do the job. Election by a majority of votes and strict accountability to the electors was not essential. Constituencies did not instruct their members, and election promises were unknown. Members 'were elected to bind their constituents, and not to be bound by them'.³⁵ It is not too fanciful to suggest that some of these features are reproduced in modern trade unions, though, of course, with many profound differences. One of these is that trade union officials do not undertake an onerous unpaid job, but enter on a remunerative career. This remark is not meant to be offensive, and, indeed, it would hardly be seemly for a university professor to criticise a public institution on the ground that its affairs are managed largely by its salaried employees.

All that I have said so far has been by way of introduction to my main task. I have not tried to put before you new facts culled by laborious research. The limit of my ambition has been to regroup familiar facts in a pattern which may make them appear to some of you in a new light. I thought it necessary to do this in order to prepare the ground for the more difficult, speculative and controversial study of the contemporary scene, in which the leading role is played by the social rights of citizenship. It is to the impact of these on social class that I must now turn my attention.

4. Social Rights in the Twentieth Century

The period of which I have hitherto been speaking was one during which the growth of citizenship, substantial and impressive though it was, had little direct effect on social inequality. Civil rights gave legal powers whose use was drastically curtailed by class prejudice and lack of economic opportunity. Political rights gave potential power whose exercise demanded experience, organisation and a change of ideas as to the proper functions of government. All these took time to develop. Social rights were at a minimum and were not woven into the fabric of citizenship. The common purpose of statutory and voluntary effort was to abate the nuisance of poverty without disturbing the pattern of inequality of which poverty was the most obviously unpleasant consequence.

A new period opened at the end of the nineteenth century, conveniently marked by Booth's survey of Life and Labour of the People in London and the Royal Commission on the Aged Poor. It saw the first big advance in social rights, and this involved significant changes in the egalitarian principles expressed in citizenship. But there were other forces at work as well. A rise of money incomes unevenly distributed over the social classes altered the economic distance which separated these classes from one another, diminishing the gap between skilled and unskilled labour and between skilled labour and non-manual workers, while the steady increase in small savings blurred the class distinction between the capitalist and the propertyless proletarian. Secondly, a system of direct taxation, ever more steeply graduated, compressed the whole scale of disposable incomes. Thirdly, mass production for the home market and a growing interest on the part of industry in the needs and tastes of the common people enabled the less well-to-do to enjoy a material civilisation which differed less markedly in quality from that of the rich than it had ever done before. All this profoundly altered the setting in which the progress of citizenship took place. Social integration spread from the sphere of sentiment and patriotism into that of material enjoyment. The components of a civilised and cultured life, formerly the monopoly of the few, were brought progressively within reach of the many, who were encouraged thereby to stretch out their hands towards those that still eluded their grasp. The diminution of inequality strengthened the demand for its abolition, at least with regard to the essentials of social welfare.

These aspirations have in part been met by incorporating social rights in the status of citizenship and thus creating a universal right to real income which is not proportionate to the market value of the claimant. Class-abatement is still the aim of social rights, but it has acquired a new meaning. It is no longer merely an attempt to abate the obvious nuisance of destitution in the lowest ranks of society. It has assumed the guise of action modifying the whole pattern of social inequality. It is no longer content to raise the floor-level in the basement of the social edifice, leaving the superstructure as it was. It has begun to remodel the whole building, and it might even end by converting a skyscraper into a bungalow. It is therefore important to consider whether any such ultimate aim is implicit in the nature of this development, or whether, as I put it at the outset, there are natural limits to the contemporary drive towards greater social and economic equality. To answer this question I must survey and analyse the social services of the twentieth century.

I said earlier that the attempts made to remove the barriers between civil rights and their remedies gave evidence of a new attitude towards the problem of equality. I can therefore conveniently begin my survey by looking at the latest example of such an attempt, the Legal Aid and Advice Bill, which offers a social service designed to strengthen the civil right of the citizen to settle his disputes in a court of law. It also brings us face to face at once with one of the major issues of our problem, the possibility of combining in one system the two principles of social justice and market price. The state is not prepared to make the administration of justice free for all. One reason for this—though not, of course, the only one—is that costs perform a useful function by discouraging frivolous litigation and encouraging the acceptance of reasonable settlements. If all actions which are started went to trial, the machinery of justice would break down. Also, the amount that it is appropriate to spend on a case depends largely on what it is worth to the parties, and of this, it is argued, they themselves are the only judges. It is very different in a health service, where the seriousness of the disease and the nature of the treatment required can be objectively assessed with very little reference to the importance the patient attaches to it. Nevertheless, though some payment is demanded, it must not take a form which deprives the litigant of his right to justice or puts him at a disadvantage vis-a-vis his opponent.

The main provisions of the scheme are as follows. The service will be confined to an economic class—those whose disposable income and capital do not exceed £420 and £500 respectively.[36] 'Disposable' means the balance after considerable deductions have been allowed for dependants, rent, ownership of house and tools, and so forth. The maximum contributable by the litigant towards his own costs is limited to half the excess of his disposable income over £75. His liability towards the costs of the other side, if he loses, is entirely in the discretion of the court. He will have the professional assistance of solicitor and counsel drawn from a panel of volunteers, and they will be remunerated for their services, in the High Court (and above) at rates 15 per cent below what the Taxing Master would regard as reasonable in the free market, and in the County Court according to uniform scales not yet fixed.

The scheme, it will be seen, makes use of the principles of the income limit and the means test, which have just been abandoned in the other major social services. And the means test will be applied, or the maximum contribution assessed, by the National Assistance Board, whose officers, in addition to making the allowances prescribed in the regulations, 'will have general discretionary powers to enable them to deduct from income any sums which they normally disregard in dealing with an application for assistance under the National Assistance Act, 1948'.[37]

It will be interesting to see whether this link with the old Poor Law will make Legal Aid unsavoury to many of those entitled to avail themselves of it, who will include persons with gross incomes up to £600 or £700 a year. But, quite apart from the agents employed to enforce it, the reason for introducing a means test is clear. The price payable for the service of the court and of the legal profession plays a useful part by testing the urgency of the demand. It is, therefore, to be retained. But the impact of price on demand is to be made less unequal by adjusting the bill to the income out of which it must be met. The method of adjustment resembles the operation of a progressive tax. If we consider income only, and ignore capital, we see that a man with a disposable income of £200 would be liable to contribute £22, or 11 per cent of that income, and a man with a disposable income of £420 would have a maximum contribution of £132, or over 31 per cent of that income.

A system of this kind may work quite well (assuming the scale of adjustment to be satisfactory) provided the market price of the service is a reasonable one for the smallest income that does not qualify for assistance. Then the price scale can taper down from this pivotal point until it vanishes where the income is too small to pay anything. No awkward gap will appear at the top between the assisted and the unassisted. The method is in use for state scholarships to universities. The cost to be met in this case is the standardised figure for maintenance plus fees. Deductions are made from the gross income of the parents on lines similar to those proposed for Legal Aid, except that income tax is not deducted. The resulting figure is known as the 'scale income'. This is applied to a table which shows the parental contribution at each point on the scale. Scale incomes up to £600 pay nothing, and the ceiling above which parents must pay the full costs, without subsidy, is £1,500. A Working Party has recently recommended that the ceiling should be raised 'to at least £2,000' (before tax), [38] which is a fairly generous poverty line for a social service. It is not unreasonable to assume that, at that income level, the market cost of a university education can be met by the family without undue hardship.

The Legal Aid Scheme will probably work in much the same way for County Court cases, where costs are moderate. Those with incomes at the top of the scale will not normally receive any subsidy towards their own costs, even if they lose their case. The contribution they can be called on to make out of their own funds will usually be enough to cover them. They will thus be in the same position as those just outside the scheme, and no awkward gap will appear. Litigants coming within the scheme will, however, get professional legal assistance at a controlled and reduced price, and that is in itself a valuable privilege. But in a heavy

High Court case the maximum contribution of the man at the top of the scale would be far from sufficient to meet his own costs if he was defeated. His liability under the scheme could, therefore, be many times less than that of a man, just outside the scheme, who fought and lost an identical action. In such cases the gap may be very noticeable, and this is particularly serious in litigation, which takes the form of a contest. The contest may be between an assisted litigant and an unassisted one, and they will be fighting under different rules. One will be protected by the principle of social justice, while the other is left to the mercy of the market and the ordinary obligations imposed by contract and the rules of the court. A measure of class-abatement may, in some cases, create a form of class privilege. Whether this will happen depends largely on the content of regulations which have not yet been issued, and on the way in which the court uses its discretion in awarding costs against assisted litigants who lose their actions.

This particular difficulty could be overcome if the system were made universal, or nearly so, by carrying the scale of maximum contributions up to much higher income levels. In other words, the means test could be preserved, but the income limit dropped. But this would mean bringing all, or practically all, legal practitioners into the scheme, and subjecting them to controlled prices for their services. It would amount almost to the nationalisation of the profession, so far as litigation is concerned, or so it would probably appear to the barristers, whose profession is inspired by a strong spirit of individualism. And the disappearance of private practice would deprive the Taxing Masters of a standard by which to fix the controlled price.

I have chosen this example to illustrate some of the difficulties that arise when one tries to combine the principles of social equality and the price system.Differential price adjustment by scale to different incomes is one method of doing this. It was widely used by doctors and hospitals until the National Health Service made this unnecessary. It frees real income, in certain forms, from its dependence on money income. If the principle were universally applied, differences in money income would become meaningless. The same result could be achieved by making all gross incomes equal, or by reducing unequal gross incomes to equal net incomes by taxation. Both processes have been going on, up to a point. Both are checked by the need to preserve differential incomes as a source of economic incentive. But, when different methods of doing much the same thing are combined, it may be possible to carry the process much further without upsetting the economic machine, because their various consequences are not easily added together, and the total effect may escape notice in the general confusion. And we must remember that gross money incomes provide the measuring-rod by which we traditionally assess social and economic achievement and prestige. Even if they lost all meaning in terms of real income, they might still function, like orders and decorations, as spurs to effort and badges of success. But I must return to my survey of the social services. The most familiar principle in use is not, of course, the scaled price (which I have just been discussing), but the guaranteed minimum. The state guarantees a minimum supply of certain essential goods and services (such as medical attention and supplies, shelter and education) or a minimum money income available to be spent on essentials–as in the case of old age pensions, insurance benefits and family allowances. Anyone able to exceed the guaranteed minimum out of his own resources is at liberty to do so. Such a system looks, on the face of it, like a more generous version of class-abatement in its original form. It raises the floor-level at the bottom, but does not automatically flatten the superstructure. But its effects need closer examination.

The degree of equalisation achieved depends on four things–whether the benefit is offered to all or to a limited class; whether it takes the form of money payment or service rendered; whether the minimum is high or low; and how the money to pay for the benefit is raised. Cash benefits subject to income limit and means test had a simple and obvious equalising effect. They achieved class-abatement in the early and limited sense of the term. The aim was to ensure that all citizens should attain at least to the prescribed minimum, either by their own resources or with assistance if they could not do it without. The benefit was given onl to those who needed it, and thus inequalities at the bottom of the scale were ironed out. The system operated in its simplest and most unadulterated form in the case of the Poor Law and old age pensions. But economic equalisation might be accompanied by psychological class discrimination. The stigma which attached to the Poor Law made 'pauper' a derogatory term defining a class. 'Old age pensioner' may have had a little of the same flavour, but without the taint of shame.

The general effect of social insurance, when confined to an income group, was similar. It differed in that there was no means test. Contribution gave a right to benefit. But, broadly speaking, the income of the group was raised by the excess of benefits over total expenditure by the group in contributions and additional taxes, and the income gap between this group and those above it was thereby reduced. The exact effect is hard to estimate, because of the wide range of incomes within the group and the varying incidence of the risks covered. When the scheme was extended to all, this gap was reopened, though again we have to take account of the combined effects of the regressive flat-rate levy and the, in part, progressive taxation which contributed to the financing of the scheme. Nothing will induce me to embark on a discussion of this problem. But a total scheme is less specifically class-abating in a purely economic sense than a limited one, and social insurance is less so than a means-test service. Flat-rate benefits do not reduce the gaps between different incomes. Their equalising effect depends on the fact that they make a bigger percentage addition to small incomes than to large. And, even though the concept of diminishing marginal utility (if one may still refer to it) can strictly be applied only to the rising income of one unchanging individual, that remains a matter of some significance. When a free service, as in the case of health, is extended from a limited income group to the whole population, the direct effect is in part to increase the inequality of disposable incomes, again subject to modification by the incidence of taxes. For members of the middle classes, who used to pay their doctors, find this part of their income released for expenditure on other things.

I have been skating gingerly over this very thin ice in order to make one point. The extension of the social services is not primarily a means of equalising incomes. In some cases it may, in others it may not. The question is relatively unimportant; it belongs to a different department of social policy. What matters is that there is a general enrichment of the concrete substance of civilised life, a general reduction of risk and insecurity, an equalisation between the more and the less fortunate at all levels–between the healthy and the sick, the employed and the unemployed, the old and the active, the bachelor and the father of a large family. Equalisation is not so much between classes as between individuals within a population which is now treated for this purpose as though it were one class. Equality of status is more important than equality of income.

Even when benefits are paid in cash, this class fusion is outwardly expressed in the form of a new common experience. All learn what it means to have an insurance card that must be regularly stamped (by somebody), or to collect children's allowances or pensions from the post office. But where the benefit takes the form of a service, the qualitative element enters into the benefit itself, and not only into the process by which it is obtained. The extension of such services can therefore have a profound effect on the qualitative aspects of social differentiation. The old elementary schools, though open to all, were used by a social class (admittedly a very large and varied one) for which no other kind of education was available. Its members were brought up in segregation from the higher classes and under influences which set their stamp on the children subjected to them. 'Ex-elementary schoolboy' became a label which a man might carry through life, and it pointed to a distinction which was real, and not merely conventional, in character. For a divided educational system, by promoting both intra-class similarity and inter-class difference, gave emphasis and precision to a criterion of social distance. As Professor Tawney has said, translating the views of educationalists into his own inimitable prose: 'The intrusion into educational organisation of the vulgarities of the class system is an irrelevance as mischievous in effect as it is odious in conception.'[39] The limited service was class-making at the same time as it was class-abating. Today the segregation still takes place, but subsequent education, available to all, makes it possible for a re-sorting to take place. I shall have to consider in a moment whether class intrudes in a different way into this re-sorting.

Similarly the early health service added 'panel patient' to our vocabulary of social class, and many members of the middle classes are now learning exactly what the term signifies. But the extension of the service has reduced the social importance of the distinction. The common experience offered by a general health service embraces all but a small minority at the top and spreads across the important class barriers in the middle ranks of the hierarchy. At the same time the guaranteed minimum has been raised to such a height that the term 'minimum' becomes a misnomer. The intention, at least, is to make it approximate so nearly to the reasonable maximum that the extras which the rich are still able to buy will be no more than frills and luxuries. The provided service, not the purchased service, becomes the norm of social welfare. Some people think that, in such circumstances, the independent sector cannot survive for long. If it disappears, the skyscraper will have been converted into a bungalow. If the present system continues and attains its ideals, the result might be described as a bungalow surmounted by an architecturally insignificant turret.

Benefits in the form of a service have this further characteristic that the rights of the citizen cannot be precisely defined. The qualitative element is too great. A modicum of legally enforceable rights may be granted, but what matters to the citizen is the superstructure of legitimate expectations. It may be fairly easy to enable every child below a certain age to spend the required number of hours in school. It is much harder to satisfy the legitimate expectation that the education should be given by trained teachers in classes of moderate size. It may be possible for every citizen who wishes it to be registered with a doctor. It is much harder to ensure that his ailments will be properly cared for. And so we find that legislation, instead of being the decisive step that puts policy into immediate effect, acquires more and more the character of a declaration of policy that is hoped to put into effect some day. We think at once of county colleges and health centres. The rate of progress depends on the magnitude of the national resources and their distribution between competing claims. Nor can the state easily foresee what it will cost to fulfil its obligations, for, as the standard expected of the service rises–as it inevitably must in a progressive society–the obligations automatically get heavier. The target is perpetually moving forward, and the state may never be able to get quite within range of it. It follows that individual rights must be subordinated to national plans.

Expectations officially recognised as legitimate are not claims that must be met in each case when presented. They become, as it were, details in a design for community living. The obligation of the state is towards society as a whole, whose remedy in case of default lies in parliament or a local council, instead of to individual citizens, whose remedy lies in a court of law, or at least in a quasi-judicial tribunal. The maintenance of a fair balance between these collective and individual elements in social rights is a matter of vital importance to the democratic socialist state.

The point I have just made is clearest in the case of housing. Here the tenure of existing dwellings has been protected by firm legal rights, enforceable in a court of law. The system has become very complicated, because it has grown piecemeal, and it cannot be maintained that the benefits are equally distributed in proportion to real need. But the basic right of the individual citizen to have a dwelling at all is minimal. He can claim no more than a roof over his head, and his claim can be met, as we have seen in recent years, by a shake-down in a disused cinema converted into a rest centre. Nevertheless, the general obligation of the state towards society collectively with regard to housing is one of the heaviest it has to bear. Public policy has unequivocally given the citizen a legitimate expectation of a home fit for a family to live in, and the promise is not now confined to heroes. It is true that, in dealing with individual claims, authorities work as far as possible on a priority scale of needs. But, when a slum is being cleared, an old city remodelled, or a new town planned, individual claims must be subordinated to the general programme of social advance. An element of chance, and therefore of inequality, enters. One family may be moved ahead of its turn into a model dwelling, because it is part of a community due for early treatment. A second will have to wait, although its physical conditions may be worse than those of the first. As the work goes on, though in many places inequalities vanish, in others they become more apparent. Let me give you one small example of this. In the town of Middlesbrough, part of the population of a blighted area had been moved to a new housing estate. It was found that, among the children living on this estate, one in eight of those who competed for places in secondary schools were successful. Among the section of the same original population that had been left behind the proportion was one in 154.[40] The contrast is so staggering that one hesitates to offer any precise explanation of it, but it remains a striking example of inequality between individuals appearing as the interim result of the progressive satisfaction of collective social rights. Eventually, when the housing programme has been completed, such inequalities should disappear.

There is another aspect of housing policy which, I believe, implies the intrusion of a new element into the rights of citizenship. It comes into play when the design for living, to which I have said individual rights must be subordinated, is not limited to one section at the bottom of the social scale nor to one particular type of need, but covers the general aspects of the life of a whole community. Town planning is total planning in this sense. Not only does it treat the community as a whole, but it affects and must take account of all social activities, customs and interests. It aims at creating new physical environments which will actively foster the growth of new human societies. It must decide what these societies are to be like, and try to provide for all the major diversities which they ought to contain. Town planners are fond of talking about a 'balanced community' as their objective. This means a society that contains a proper mixture of all social classes, as well as of age and sex groups, occupations and so forth. They do not want to build working-class neighbourhoods and middle-class neighbourhoods, but they do propose to build working-class houses and middle-class houses. Their aim is not a classless society, but a society in which class differences are legitimate in terms of social justice, and in which, therefore, the classes cooperate more closely than at present to the common benefit of all. When a planning authority decides that it needs a larger middle-class element in its town (as it very often does) and makes designs to meet its needs and fit its standards, it is not, like a speculative builder, merely responding to a commercial demand. It must reinterpret the demand in harmony with its total plan and then give it the sanction of its authority as the responsible organ of a community of citizens. The middle-class man can then say, not 'I will come if you pay the price I feel strong enough to demand', but 'If you want me as a citizen, you must give me the status which is due as of right to the kind of citizen I am.' This is one example of the way in which citizenship is itself becoming the architect of social inequality.

The second, and more important, example is in the field of education, which also illustrates my earlier point about the balance between individual and collective social rights. In the first phase of our public education, rights were minimal and equal. But, as we have observed, a duty was attached to the right, not merely because the citizen has a duty to himself, as well as a right, to develop all that is in him–a duty which neither the child nor the parent may fully appreciate–but because society recognised that it needed an educated population. In fact the nineteenth century has been accused of regarding elementary education solely as a means of providing capitalist employers with more valuable workers, and higher education merely as an instrument to increase the power of the nation to compete with its industrial rivals. And you may have noticed that recent studies of educational opportunity in the pre-war years have been concerned to reveal the magnitude of social waste quite as much as to protest against the frustration of natural human rights.

In the second phase of our educational history, which began in 1902, the educational ladder was officially accepted as an important, though still small, part of the system. But the balance between collective and individual rights remained much the same. The state decided what it could afford to spend on free secondary and higher education, and the children competed for the limited number of places provided. There was no pretence that all who could benefit from more advanced education would get it, and there was no recognition of any absolute natural right to be educated according to one's capacities. But in the third phase, which started in 1944, individual rights have ostensibly been given priority. Competition for scarce places is to be replaced by selection and distribution into appropriate places, sufficient in number to accommodate all, at least at the secondary school level. In the Act of 1944 there is a passage which says that the supply of secondary schools will not be considered adequate unless they 'afford for all pupils opportunities for education offering such variety of instruction and training as may be desirable in view of their different ages, abilities and aptitudes'. Respect for individual rights could hardly be more strongly expressed. Yet I wonder whether it will work out like that in practice.

If it were possible for the school system to treat the pupil entirely as an end in himself, and to regard education as giving him something whose value he could enjoy to the full whatever his station in after-life, then it might be possible to mould the educational plan to the shape demanded by individual needs, regardless of any other considerations. But, as we all know, education today is closely linked with occupation, and one, at least, of the values the pupil expects to get from it is a qualification for employment at an appropriate level. Unless great changes take place, it seems likely that the educational plan will be adjusted to occupational demand. The proportion between Grammar, Technical and Modern Secondary Schools cannot well be fixed without reference to the proportion between jobs of corresponding grades. And a balance between the two systems may have to be sought in justice to the pupil himself. For if a boy who is given a Grammar School education can then get nothing but a Modern School job, he will cherish a grievance and feel that he has been cheated. It is highly desirable that this attitude should change, so that a boy in such circumstances will be grateful for his education and not resentful at his job. But to accomplish such a change is no easy task.

I see no signs of any relaxation of the bonds that tie education to occupation. On the contrary, they appear to be growing stronger. Great and increasing respect is paid to certificates, matriculation, degrees and diplomas as qualifications for employment, and their freshness does not fade with the passage of the years. A man of 40 may be judged by his performance in an examination taken at the age of 15. The ticket obtained on leaving school or college is for a life journey. The man with a third-class ticket who later feels able to claim a seat in a first-class carriage will not be admitted, even if he is prepared to pay the difference. That would not be fair to the others. He must go back to the start and re-book, by passing the prescribed examination. And it is unlikely that the state will offer to pay his return fare. This is not, of course, true of the whole field of employment, but it is a fair description of a large and significant part of it, whose extension is being constantly advocated. I have, for instance, recently read an article in which it is urged that every aspirant to an administrative or managerial post in business should be required to qualify 'by passing the matriculation or equivalent examination'.[41] This development is partly the result of the systematisation of techniques in more and more professional, semi-professional and skilled occupations, though I must confess that some of the claims of so-called professional bodies to exclusive possession of esoteric skill and knowledge appear to me to be rather thin. But it is also fostered by the refinement of the selective process within the educational system itself. The more confident the claim of education to be able to sift human material during the early years of life, the more is mobility concentrated within those years, and consequently limited thereafter.

The right of the citizen in this process of selection and mobility is the right to equality of opportunity. Its aim is to eliminate hereditary privilege. In essence it is the equal right to display and develop differences, or inequalities; the equal right to be recognised as unequal. In the early stages of the establishment of such a system the major effect is, of course, to reveal hidden equalities–to enable the poor boy to show that he is as good as the rich boy. But the final outcome is a structure of unequal status fairly apportioned to unequal abilities. The process is sometimes associated with ideas of *laissez faire* individualism, but within the educational system it is a matter, not of *laissez faire*, but of planning. The process through which abilities are revealed, the influences to which they are subjected, the tests by which they are measured, and the rights given as a result of the tests are all planned. Equality of opportunity is offered to all children entering the primary schools, but at an early age they are usually divided into three streams–the best, the average and the backward. Already opportunity is becoming unequal, and the children's range of chances limited. About the age of eleven they are tested again, probably by a team of teachers, examiners and psychologists. None of these is infallible, but perhaps sometimes three wrongs may make a right. Classification follows for distribution into the three types of secondary school. Opportunity becomes still more unequal, and the chance of further education has already been limited to a select few. Some of these, after being tested again, will go on to receive it. In the end the jumble of mixed seed originally put into the machine emerges in neatly labelled packets ready to be sown in the appropriate gardens.

I have deliberately couched this description in the language of cynicism in order to bring out the point that, however genuine may be the desire of the educational authorities to offer enough variety to satisfy all individual needs, they must, in a mass service of this kind, proceed by repeated classification into groups, and this is followed at each stage by assimilation within each group and differentiation between groups. That is precisely the way in which social classes in a fluid society have always taken shape. Differences within each class are ignored as irrelevant; differences between classes are given exaggerated significance. Thus qualities which are in reality strung out along a continuous scale are made to create a hierarchy of groups, each with its special character and status. The main features of the system are inevitable, and its advantages, in particular the elimination of inherited privilege, far outweigh its incidental defects. The latter can be attacked and kept within bounds by giving as much opportunity as possible for second thoughts about classification, both in the educational system itself and in after-life.

The conclusion of importance to my argument is that, through education in its relations with occupational structure, citizenship operates as an instrument of social stratification. There is no reason to deplore this, but we should be aware of its consequences. The status acquired by education is carried out into the world bearing the stamp of legitimacy, because it has been conferred by an institution designed to give the citizen his just rights. That which the market offers can be measured against that which the status claims. If a large discrepancy appears, the ensuing attempts to eliminate it will take the form, not of a bargain about economic value, but of a debate about social rights. And it may be that there is already a serious discrepancy between the expectations of those who reach the middle grades in education and the status of the non-manual jobs for which they are normally destined.

I said earlier that in the twentieth century citizenship and the capitalist class system have been at war. Perhaps the phrase is rather too strong, but it is quite clear that the former has imposed modifications on the latter. But we should not be justified in assuming that although status is a principle that conflicts with contract, the stratified status system which is creeping into citizenship is an alien element in the economic world outside. Social rights in their modern form imply an invasion of contract by status, the subordination of market price to social justice, the replacement of the free bargain by the declaration of rights. But are these principles quite foreign to the practice of the market today, or are they there already, entrenched within the contract system itself? I think it is clear that they are.

As I have already pointed out, one of the main achievements of political power in the nineteenth century was to clear the way for the growth of trade unionism by enabling the workers to use their civil rights collectively. This was an anomaly, because hitherto it was political rights that were used for collective action, through parliament and local councils, whereas civil rights were intensely individual, and had therefore harmonised with the individualism of early capitalism. Trade unionism created a sort of secondary industrial citizenship, which naturally became imbued with the spirit appropriate to an institution of citizenship. Collective civil rights could be used, not merely for bargaining in the true sense of the term, but for the assertion of basic rights. The position was an impossible one and could only be transitional. Rights are not a proper matter for bargaining. To have to bargain for a living wage in a society which accepts the living wage as a social right is as absurd as to have to haggle for a vote in a society which accepts the vote as a political right. Yet the early twentieth century attempted to make sense of this absurdity. It fully endorsed collective bargaining as a normal and peaceful market operation, while recognising in principle the right of the citizen to a minimum standard of civilised living, which was precisely what the trade unions believed, and with good reason, that they were trying to win for their members with the weapon of the bargain.

In the outburst of big strikes immediately before the First World War this note of a concerted demand for social rights was clearly audible. The government was forced to intervene. It professed to do so entirely for the protection of the public, and pretended not to be concerned with the issues in dispute. In 1912 Mr Askwith, the chief negotiator, told

Mr Asquith, the Prime Minister, that intervention had failed and government prestige had suffered. To which the Prime Minister replied: 'Every word you have spoken endorses the opinion I have formed. It is a degradation of government.'[42] History soon showed that such a view was a complete anachronism. The government can no longer stand aloof from industrial disputes, as though the level of wages and the standard of living of the workers were matters with which it need not concern itself. And government intervention in industrial disputes has been met from the other side by trade union intervention in the work of government. This is both a significant and a welcome development, provided its implications are fully realised. In the past trade unionism had to assert social rights by attacks delivered from outside the system in which power resided. Today it defends them from inside, in cooperation with government. On major issues crude economic bargaining is converted into something more like a joint discussion of policy.

The implication is that decisions reached in this way must command respect. If citizenship is invoked in the defence of rights, the corresponding duties of citizenship cannot be ignored. These do not require a man to sacrifice his individual liberty or to submit without question to every demand made by government. But they do require that his acts should be inspired by a lively sense of responsibility towards the welfare of the community. Trade union leaders in general accept this implication, but this is not true of all members of the rank and file. The traditions built up at a time when trade unions were fighting for their existence, and when conditions of employment depended wholly on the outcome of unequal bargaining, make its acceptance very difficult. Unofficial strikes have become very frequent, and it is clear that one important element in industrial disputes is discord between trade union leaders and certain sections of trade union members. Now duties can derive either from status or from contract. Leaders of unofficial strikes are liable to reject both. The strikes usually involve breach of contract or the repudiation of agreements. Appeal is made to some allegedly higher principle–in reality, though this may not be expressly asserted, to the status rights of industrial citizenship. There are many precedents today for the subordination of contract to status. Perhaps the most familiar are to be found in our handling of the housing problem. Rents are controlled and the rights of occupants protected after their contracts have expired, houses are requisitioned, agreements freely entered into are set aside or modified by tribunals applying the principles of social equity and the just price. The sanctity of contract gives way to the requirements of public policy, and I am not suggesting for a moment that this ought not to be so. But if the obligations of contract are brushed aside by an appeal to the rights of citizenship, then the duties of citizenship must be accepted as well. In some recent unofficial strikes an attempt has, I think, been made to claim the rights both of status and of contract while repudiating the duties under both these heads.

But my main concern is not with the nature of strikes, but rather with the current conception of what constitutes a fair wage. I think it is clear that this conception includes the notion of status. It enters into every discussion of wage rates and professional salaries. What *ought* a medical specialist or a dentist to earn, we ask? Would twice the salary of a university professor be about right, or is that not enough? And, of course, the system envisaged is one of stratified, not uniform, status. The claim is not merely for a basic living wage with such variations above that level as can be extracted by each grade from the conditions in the market at the moment. The claims of status are to a hierarchical wage structure, each level of which represents a social right and not merely a market value. Collective bargaining must involve, even in its elementary forms, the classification of workers into groups, or grades, within which minor occupational differences are ignored. As in mass schooling, so in mass employment, questions of rights, standards, opportunities and so forth can be intelligibly discussed and handled only in terms of a limited number of categories and by cutting up a continuous chain of differences into a series of classes whose names instantly ring the appropriate bell in the mind of the busy official. As the area of negotiation spreads, the assimilation of groups necessarily follows on the assimilation of individuals, until the stratification of the whole population of workers is, as far as possible, standardised. Only then can general principles of social justice be formulated. There must be uniformity within each grade, and difference between grades. These principles dominate the minds of those discussing wage claims, even though rationalisation produces other arguments, such as that profits are excessive and the industry can afford to pay higher wages, or that higher wages are necessary to maintain the supply of suitable labour or to prevent its decline.

The White Paper on Personal Incomes[43] flashed a beam of light into these dark places of the mind, but the end result has been only to make the process of rationalisation more intricate and laborious. The basic conflict between social rights and market value has not been resolved. One labour spokesman said: 'An equitable relationship must be established between industry and industry.'[44] An equitable relationship is a social, not an economic, concept. The General Council of the TUC approved the principles of the White Paper to the extent that 'they recognize the need to safeguard those wage differentials which are essential elements in the wages structure of many important industries, and are required to sustain those standards of craftsmanship, training and experience that contribute directly to industrial efficiency and higher productivity.'[45] Here market value and economic incentive find a place in an argument which is fundamentally concerned with status. The White Paper itself took a rather different, and possibly a truer, view of differentials. 'The last hundred years have seen the growth of certain traditional or customary relationships between personal incomes–including wages and salaries–in different occupations…These have no necessary relevance to modern conditions.' Tradition and custom are social, not economic, principles, and they are old names for the modern structure of status rights.

The White Paper stated frankly that differentials based on these social concepts could not satisfy current economic requirements. They did not provide the incentives needed to secure the best distribution of labour. 'Relative income levels must be such as to encourage the movement of labour to those industries where it is most needed, and should not, as in some cases they still do, tempt it in a contrary direction.' Notice that it says '*still* do'. Once again the modern conception of social rights is treated as a survival from the dark past. As we go on, the confusion thickens. 'Each claim for an increase in wages or salaries must be considered on its national merits', that is, in terms of national policy. But this policy cannot be directly enforced by the exercise of the political rights of citizenship through government, because that would involve 'an incursion by the Government into what has hitherto been regarded as a field of free contract between individuals and organizations', that is, an invasion of the civil rights of the citizen. Civil rights are therefore to assume political responsibility, and free contract is to act as the instrument of national policy. And there is yet another paradox. The incentive that operates in the free contract system of the open market is the incentive of personal gain. The incentive that corresponds to social rights is that of public duty. To which is the appeal being made? The answer is, to both. The citizen is urged to respond to the call of duty by allowing some scope to the motive of individual self-interest. But these paradoxes are not the invention of muddled brains; they are inherent in our contemporary social system. And they need not cause us undue anxiety, for a little common sense can often move a mountain of paradox in the world of action, though logic may be unable to surmount it in the world of thought.

5. Conclusions

I have tried to show how citizenship, and other forces outside it, have been altering the pattern of social inequality. To complete the picture I ought now to survey the results as a whole on the structure of social class. They have undoubtedly been profound, and it may be that the inequalities permitted, and even moulded, by citizenship do not any longer constitute class distinctions in the sense in which that term is used for past societies. But to examine this question I should require another lecture, and it would probably consist of a mixture of dry statistics of uncertain meaning and meaningful judgements of doubtful validity. For our ignorance of this matter is profound. It is therefore perhaps fortunate for the reputation of sociology that I should be obliged to confine myself to a few tentative observations, made in an attempt to answer the four questions which I posed at the end of my introduction to my theme. We have to look for the combined effects of three factors. First, the compression, at both ends, of the scale of income distribution. Second, the great extension of the area of common culture and common experience. And third, the enrichment of the universal status of citizenship, combined with the recognition and stabilisation of certain status differences chiefly through the linked systems of education and occupation. The first two have made the third possible. Status differences can receive the stamp of legitimacy in terms of democratic citizenship provided they do not cut too deep, but occur within a population united in a single civilisation; and provided they are not an expression of hereditary privilege. This means that inequalities can be tolerated within a fundamentally egalitarian society provided they are not dynamic, that is to say that they do not create incentives which spring from dissatisfaction and the feeling that 'this kind of life is not good enough for me', or 'I am determined that my son shall be spared what I had to put up with'. But the kind of inequality pleaded for in the White Paper can be justified only if it *is* dynamic, and if it *does* provide an incentive to change and betterment. It may prove, therefore, that the inequalities permitted, and even moulded, by citizenship will not function in an economic sense as forces influencing the free distribution of manpower. Or that social stratification persists, but social ambition ceases to be a normal phenomenon, and becomes a deviant behaviour pattern–to use some of the jargon of sociology.

Should things develop to such lengths, we might find that the only remaining drive with a consistent distributive effect–distributive, that is, of manpower through the hierarchy of economic levels–was the ambition of the schoolboy to do well in his lessons, to pass his examinations, and to win promotion up the educational ladder. And if the official aim of securing 'parity of esteem' between the three types of secondary school were realised, we might lose the greater part even of that. Such would be the extreme result of establishing social conditions in which every man was content with the station of life to which it had pleased citizenship to call him.

In saying this I have answered two of my four questions, the first and the last. I asked whether the sociological hypothesis latent in Marshall's essay is valid today, the hypothesis, namely, that there is a kind of basic human equality, associated with full community membership, which is not inconsistent with a superstructure of economic inequality. I asked, too, whether there was any limit to the present drive towards social equality inherent in the principles governing the movement. My answer is that the preservation of economic inequalities has been made more difficult by the enrichment of the status of citizenship. There is less room for them, and there is more and more likelihood of their being challenged. But we are certainly proceeding at present on the assumption that the hypothesis is valid. And this assumption provides the answer to the second question. We are not aiming at absolute equality. There are limits inherent in the egalitarian movement. But the movement is a double one. It operates partly through citizenship and partly through the economic system. In both cases the aim is to remove inequalities which cannot be regarded as legitimate, but the standard of legitimacy is different. In the former it is the standard of social justice, in the latter it is social justice combined with economic necessity. It is possible, therefore, that the inequalities permitted by the two halves of the movement will not coincide. Class distinctions may survive which have no appropriate economic function, and economic differences which do not correspond with accepted class distinctions.

My third question referred to the changing balance between rights and duties. Rights have been multiplied, and they are precise. Each individual knows just what he is entitled to claim. The duty whose discharge is most obviously and immediately necessary for the fulfilment of the right is the duty to pay taxes and insurance contributions. Since these are compulsory, no act of will is involved, and no keen sentiment of loyalty. Education and military service are also compulsory. The other duties are vague, and are included in the general obligation to live the life of a good citizen, giving such service as one can to promote the welfare of the community. But the community is so large that the obligation appears remote and unreal. Of paramount importance is the duty to work, but the effect of one man's labour on the well-being of the whole society is so infinitely small that it is hard for him to believe that he can do much harm by withholding or curtailing it.

When social relations were dominated by contract, the duty to work was not recognised. It was a man's own affair whether he worked or not. If he chose to live idly in poverty, he was at liberty to do so, provided he did not become a nuisance. If he was able to live idly in comfort, he was regarded, not as a drone, but as an aristocrat–to be envied and admired. When the economy of this country was in process of transformation into a system of this kind, great anxiety was felt whether the necessary labour would be forthcoming. The driving forces of group custom and regulation had to be replaced by the incentive of personal gain, and grave doubts were expressed whether this incentive could be relied upon. This explains Colquhoun's views on poverty, and the pithy remark of Mandeville, that labourers 'have nothing to stir them up to be serviceable but their wants, which it is prudence to relieve but folly to cure'.[46] And in the eighteenth century their wants were very simple. They were governed by established class habits of living, and no continuous scale of rising standards of consumption existed to entice the labourers to earn more in order to spend more on desirable things hitherto just beyond their reach–like radio sets, bicycles, cinemas or holidays by the sea. The following comment by a writer in 1728, which is but one example from many in the same sense, may well have been based on sound observation. 'People in low life', he said, 'who work only for their daily bread, if they can get it by three days work in the week, will many of them make holiday the other three, or set their own price on their labour.'[47] And, if they adopted the latter course, it was generally assumed that they would spend the extra money on drink, the only easily available luxury. The general rise in the standard of living has caused this phenomenon, or something like it, to reappear in contemporary society, though cigarettes now play a more important role than drink.

It is no easy matter to revive the sense of the personal obligation to work in a new form in which it is attached to the status of citizenship. It is not made any easier by the fact that the essential duty is not to have a job and hold it, since that is relatively simple in conditions of full employment, but to put one's heart into one's job and work hard. For the standard by which to measure hard work is immensely elastic. A successful appeal to the duties of citizenship can be made in times of emergency, but the Dunkirk spirit cannot be a permanent feature of any civilisation. Nevertheless, an attempt is being made by trade union leaders to inculcate a sense of this general duty. At a conference on 18 November of last year Mr Tanner referred to 'the imperative obligation on both sides of industry to make their full contribution to the rehabilitation of the national economy and world recovery'.[48] But the national community is too large and remote to command this kind of loyalty and to make of it a continual driving force. That is why many people think that the solution of our problem lies in the development of more limited loyalties, to the local community and especially to the working group. In this latter form industrial citizenship, devolving its obligations down to the basic units of production, might supply some of the vigour that citizenship in general appears to lack.

I come finally to the second of my original four questions, which was not, however, so much a question as a statement. I pointed out that Marshall stipulated that measures designed to raise the general level of civilisation of the workers must not interfere with the freedom of the market. If they did, they might become indistinguishable from socialism. And I said that obviously this limitation on policy had since been abandoned. Socialist measures in Marshall's sense have been accepted by all political parties. This led me to the platitude that the conflict between egalitarian measures and the free market must be examined in the course of any attempt to carry Marshall's sociological hypothesis over into the modern age.

I have touched on this vast subject at several points, and in this concluding summary I will confine myself to one aspect of the problem. The unified civilisation which makes social inequalities acceptable, and threatens to make them economically functionless, is achieved by a progressive divorce between real and money incomes. This is, of course, explicit in the major social services, such as health and education, which give benefits in kind without any *ad hoc* payment. In scholarships and legal aid, prices scaled to money incomes keep real income relatively constant, in so far as it is affected by these particular needs. Rent restriction, combined with security of tenure, achieves a similar result by different means. So, in varying degrees, do rationing, food subsidies, utility goods and price controls. The advantages obtained by having a larger money income do not disappear, but they are confined to a limited area of consumption.

I spoke just now of the conventional hierarchy of the wage structure. Here importance is attached to differences in money income and the higher earnings are expected to yield real and substantial advantages–as, of course, they still do in spite of the trend towards the equalisation of real incomes. But the importance of wage differentials is, I am sure, partly symbolic. They operate as labels attached to industrial status, not only as instruments of genuine economic stratification. And we also see signs that the acceptance of this system of economic inequality by the workers themselves–especially those fairly low down in the scale–is sometimes counteracted by claims to greater equality with respect to those forms of real enjoyment which are not paid for out of wages. Manual workers may accept it as right and proper that they should earn less money than certain clerical grades, but at the same time wage-earners may press for the same general amenities as are enjoyed by salaried employees, because these should reflect the fundamental equality of all citizens and not the inequalities of earnings or occupational grades. If the manager can get a day off for a football match, why not the workman? Common enjoyment is a common right.

Recent studies of adult and child opinion have found that, when the question is posed in general terms, there is a declining interest in the earning of big money. This is not due, I think, only to the heavy burden of progressive taxation, but to an implicit belief that society should, and will, guarantee all the essentials of a decent and secure life at every level, irrespective of the amount of money earned. In a population of secondary schoolboys examined by the Bristol Institute of Education, 86 per cent wanted an interesting job at a reasonable wage and only 9 per cent a job in which they could make a lot of money. And the average intelligence quotient of the second group was 16 points lower than that of the first.[49] In a poll conducted by the British Institute of Public Opinion, 23 per cent wanted as high wages as possible, and 73 per cent preferred security at lower wages.[50] But at any given moment, and in response to a particular question about their present circumstances, most people, one would imagine, would confess to a desire for more money than they are actually getting. Another poll, taken in November 1947, suggests that even this expectation is exaggerated. For 51 per cent said their earnings were at or above a level adequate to cover family needs, and only 45 per cent that they were inadequate. The attitude is bound to vary at different social levels. The classes which have gained most from the social services, and in which real income in general has been rising, might be expected to be less preoccupied with differences in money income. But we should be prepared to find other reactions in that section of the middle classes in which the pattern of money incomes is at the moment most markedly incoherent, while the elements of civilised living traditionally most highly prized are becoming unattainable with the money incomes available–or by any other means.

The general point is one to which Professor Robbins referred when he lectured here two years ago. 'We are following,' he said, 'a policy which is self-contradictory and self-frustrating. We are relaxing taxation and seeking, where ever possible, to introduce systems of payments which fluctuate with output. And, at the same time, our price fixing and the consequential rationing system are inspired by egalitarian principles. The result is that we get the worst of both worlds.'[51] And again: 'The belief that, in normal times, it is particularly sensible to try to mix the principles and run an egalitarian real income system side by side with an inegalitarian money income system seems to me somewhat *simpliste.*'[52] Yes, to the economist perhaps, if he tries to judge the situation according to the logic of a market economy. But not necessarily to the sociologist, who remembers that social behaviour is not governed by logic, and that a human society can make a square meal out of a stew of paradox without getting indigestion–at least for quite a long time. The policy, in fact, may not be *simpliste* at all, but subtle; a newfangled application of the old maxim *divide et impera*–play one off against the other to keep the peace. But, more seriously, the word *simpliste* suggests that the antinomy is merely the result of the muddled thinking of our rulers and that, once they see the light, there is nothing to prevent them altering their line of action. I believe, on the contrary, that this conflict of principles springs from the very roots of our social order in the present phase of the development of democratic citizenship. Apparent inconsistencies are in fact a source of stability, achieved through a compromise which is not dictated by logic. This phase will not continue indefinitely. It may be that some of the conflicts within our social system are becoming too sharp for the compromise to achieve its purpose much longer. But, if we wish to assist in their resolution, we must try to understand their deeper nature and to realise the profound and disturbing effects which would be produced by any hasty attempt to reverse present and recent trends. It has been my aim in these lectures to throw a little light on one element which I believe to be of fundamental importance, namely the impact of a rapidly developing concept of the rights of citizenship on the structure of social inequality.

Notes

1. The Marshall Lectures, Cambridge 1949.
2. *Memorials of Alfred Marshall*, ed. A.C. Pigou, p. 164.
3. Ibid., p. 158.
4. Ibid., p. 37.
5. Privately printed by Thomas Tofts. The page references are to this edition.
6. Published under the title 'Prospects of Labour' in *Economica*, February, 1919.
7. *The Future of the Working Classes*, pp. 3,4.
8. Ibid., p. 6.
9. Ibid., p. 16.
10. Ibid., p. 9. The revised version of this passage is significantly different. It runs: 'The picture to be drawn will resemble in many respects those which have been shown to us by some socialists, who attributed to all men...' etc.

The condemnation is less sweeping and Marshall no longer speaks of the Socialists, en masse and with a capital 'S', in the past tense. *Memorials*, p. 109.

11. Ibid., p. 15.
12. Ibid., p. 5.
13. By this terminology, what economists sometimes call 'income from civil rights' would be called 'income from social rights'. Cf. H. Dalton, *Some Aspects of the Inequality of Incomes in Modern Communities*, Part 3, Chapters 3 and 4.
14. F. Maitland, *Constitutional History of England*, p. 105.
15. A.F. Pollard, *Evolution of Parliament*, p. 25.
16. The most important exception is the right to strike, but the conditions which made this right vital for the workman and acceptable to political opinion had not yet fully come into being.
17. G.M. Trevelyan: *English Social History*, p. 351.
18. City of London Case, 1610. See E.F. Heckscher *Mercantilism*, vol. I, pp. 269-325, where the whole story is told in considerable detail.
19. *King's Bench Reports* (Holt), p. 1002.
20. Heckscher, *Mercantilism*, vol. I, p. 283.
21. Ibid., p. 316.
22. Sidney and Beatrice Webb, *History of Trade Unionism* (1920), p. 60.
23. R.H. Tawney, *The Agrarian Problem in the Sixteenth Century* (1916), pp. 43–4.
24. *Our Partnership*, p. 79.
25. See the admirable characterisation given by R.H. Tawney in *Equality*, pp. 121–2.
26. *A Treatise on Indigence* (1806), pp. 7–8.
27. H.S. Maine, *Ancient Law* (1878), p. 170.
28. Ibid., p. 365.
29. M. Ginsberg *Studies in Sociology*, p. 171.
30. The Austin Jones Committee on County Court Procedure and the Evershed Committee on Supreme Court Practice and Procedure. The report of the former and an interim report of the latter have since been published.
31. The Rushcliffe Committee on Legal Aid and Legal Advice in England and Wales.
32. C. Grant Robertson, *England under the Hanoverians*, p. 491.
33. R.W. Pollard, *The Evolution of Parliament*, p. 155.
34. Ibid., p. 165.
35. Ibid., p. 152.
36. Where disposable capital exceeds £500, legal aid may still be granted, at the discretion of the local committee, if disposable income does not exceed £420.
37. Cmd. 7563: Summary of the Proposed New Service, p. 7, para. 17.
38. Ministry of Education, *Report of the Working Party on University Awards*, 1948, para. 60. The general account of the present system is taken from the same source.

39. R.H. Tawney, *Secondary Education for All*, p. 64.
40. Ruth Glass, *The Social Background of a Plan*, p. 129.
41. J.A. Bowie, in *Industry* (January 1949), p. 17.
42. Lord Askwith, *Industrial Problems and Disputes*, p. 228.
43. Cmd. 7321, 1948.
44. As reported in *The Times*.
45. Recommendations of the Special Committee on the Economic Situation as accepted by the General Council at their Special Meeting on 18 February 1948.
46. B. Mandeville, *The Fable of the Bees*, 6th ed. (1732), p. 213.
47. E.S. Furniss, *The Position of the Laborer in a System of Nationalism*, p. 125.
48. *The Times*, 19 November 1948.
49. *Research Bulletin*, No. 11, p. 23.
50. January 1946.
51. L. Robbins, *The Economic Problem in Peace and War*, p. 9.
52. Ibid., p. 16.

Part II
Citizenship and Social Class, Forty Years On
Tom Bottomore

1. Citizens, Classes and Equality

T.H. Marshall's lectures, given at Cambridge in 1949 and published in an expanded version the following year (Marshall 1950, reprinted above), made a very original contribution to sociological conceptions and theories of social class, and at the same time to the debates about the emerging post-war welfare state. In both spheres the concept of citizenship had a central place in his argument. Starting out from Alfred Marshall's paper (1873) on 'the future of the working classes'–according to which a certain degree of equality would be attained when, as a consequence of the reduction of heavy and excessive labour, along with greatly improved access to education and to the rights of citizenship, all men became 'gentlemen'–he proposed to substitute for the world 'gentlemen' the word 'civilised' and to interpret the claim to a civilised life as a claim to share in the social heritage, to be fully accepted as a citizen.

The argument was then pursued, initially, through an examination of the relation between citizenship and social class, in which the movement towards greater social equality was seen as the latest phase in the evolution of citizenship over several centuries, from the achievement of civil rights to the acquisition of political rights and finally social rights. This process was elegantly conceptualised in what Marshall himself referred to as a narration of events, but there was relatively little discussion of its causes, giving rise to later criticisms that it had been rather misleadingly represented as a quasi-automatic, harmonious progression to better things which was in some way immanent in the development of capitalism itself. Implicitly though, and to some extent explicitly, Marshall recognised that there were elements of conflict involved, observing that it was reasonable to expect that 'the impact of citizenship on social class should take the form of a conflict between opposing principles'. He did not, however, argue that this conflict was one between classes over the nature and content of citizenship, and he remarked indeed that 'social class occupies a secondary position in my theme'. The impact of citizenship on social classes, rather than the impact of social classes on the extension of citizenship, was clearly his principal concern.

Yet in so far as the development of citizenship in Britain from the latter part of the seventeenth century 'coincides with the rise of capitalism', it is obviously important to consider which social groups were actively engaged in, or on the other hand resisted, efforts to enlarge the rights of citizens, and more generally to bring about greater equality. From this standpoint the growth of civil rights, beginning indeed before the seventeenth century in medieval cities, can be seen as an achievement of the new bourgeoisie in conflict with dominant feudal groups of the *ancien régime*. Similarly, the extension of political rights in the nineteenth and twentieth centuries, and of social rights in the twentieth, was accomplished largely by the rapidly growing working class movement, aided by middle-class reformers, and in the case of social rights facilitated by the consequences of two world wars. Marshall himself referred to this obliquely when he observed that 'in the twentieth century citizenship and the capitalist class system have been at war', though he thought 'perhaps the phrase is rather too strong' (p. 40) and he did not pursue this aspect of his analysis.

In due course, when considering the changes that have taken place over the past 40 years, we shall need to re-examine Marshall's conception of class and of the relation between the extension of social rights, with their potential for creating a more equal society, and the economic and class system of capitalism. First, however, let us look at the second major theme of his lectures, which is the embodiment of the principle of social rights in the policies of the welfare state. He began by noting 'some of the difficulties that arise when one tries to combine the principles of social equality and the price system', and then observed that the extension of the social services was 'not primarily a means of equalising incomes', which might be tackled in other ways (see p. 61); but that what mattered was that 'there is a general enrichment of the concrete substance of civilised life, a general reduction of risk and insecurity, an equalisation between the more and the less fortunate at all levels' (p. 33). This is very close to the view expressed by R.H. Tawney in his discussion of equality (4th edn, 1952, p. 248):

> There are certain gross and crushing disabilities—conditions of life injurious to health, inferior education, economic insecurity... which place the classes experiencing them at a permanent disadvantage... There are certain services by which these crucial disabilities have been greatly mitigated, and, given time and will, can be altogether removed... The contribution to equality made by these dynamic agencies is obviously out of all proportion greater than that which would result from an annual present to every individual among the forty odd millions concerned of a sum equivalent to his quota of the total cost.

Marshall went on to note the consequences in this sense of the post-war policies in Britain, which created a national system of education and a National Health Service, and initiated a large-scale programme of house-building which included the planning of new towns. But he also pointed out that the more widely available educational opportunities tended to create a new structure of unequal status linked with unequal abilities and that 'through education in its relations with occupational structure, citizenship operates as an instrument of social stratification' (p. 39 above). Nevertheless he concluded that 'status differences can receive the stamp of legitimacy in terms of democratic citizenship provided they do not cut too deep, but occur within a population united in a single civilisation; and provided they are not an expression of hereditary privilege' (p. 44 above). Forty years later however we are still very far away from such a situation–above all in Britain, which increasingly resembles, in the view of many observers, the society of 'two nations' depicted by Disraeli–and from the widespread acceptance of 'socialist measures' in a progressive 'divorce between real and money incomes' (p. 47 above). Later, I shall examine in greater detail the post-war development of class structures and the welfare state, as well as new problems and conceptions of citizenship, drawing in part upon Marshall's own later writings on these subjects, but first it is necessary to consider some more general features of the economic and social framework in which the changes were accomplished or arrested.

2. Capitalism, Socialism and Citizenship

In 1949, in Britain, it was possible to take a fairly optimistic view of the gradual extension of citizens' rights in a democratic society which was becoming more socialist in its structure, through the nationalisation of some major sectors of the economy and the creation of a National Health Service and a system of national education, the latter regarded by many socialists as the first step towards establishing a universal system by the phasing out of private, privileged education (see, for example, the Note of Reservation by Mrs M.C. Jay to the Report of the Royal Commission on Population, June 1949). These policies, together with the priority given to creating and maintaining full employment, and proposals (which were, however, never effectively implemented) for national economic planning, were all intended to achieve equality, to a large extent by the introduction of social rights into new areas, of health, education, employment and the control of productive resources. This movement, as Marshall suggested (p. 47 above), became increasingly identified with socialism (thus going far beyond Alfred Marshall's conception of 'the amelioration of the working classes') and its main tendency was more strongly characterised by Schumpeter (1949) as a 'march into socialism'.

The drive towards equality, analysed by Schumpeter in a way which had some affinities with Marxist theory, could also be interpreted, as was done at an earlier date by Sidney Webb (1889), as the outcome of 'the irresistible progress of democracy'; and the latter view has been restated in some more recent writings (for example, Turner 1986) which see the achievement of social rights as following from the gaining of political rights by the working class and other subordinate groups. In 1949 at all events, in Britain and some other European countries, the egalitarian, mainly socialist movement may well have appeared to be an 'irresistible' tendency emerging from the development of capitalism itself, and this 'spirit of the times' no doubt influenced the way in which Marshall presented his analysis.

Just at this time, however, the world situation, and that of Britain, was beginning to change radically. In the context of the emerging cold war the American Marshall Plan for European recovery, implemented from 1948, played a major part in reviving the capitalist economies of Western Europe, notably in West Germany–although it also introduced some degree of national economic planning through the creation of the Organisation of European Economic Cooperation (OEEC, subsequently OECD) to administer the funds made available[1] – and in limiting the possibilities for any further socialist development. The Labour government in Britain, by the beginning of the 1950s, confronted increasing difficulties, due in part to its dependent relationship with the USA and exacerbated by the Korean war, which resulted in a sharp rise in the cost of imported raw materials; and in face of these difficulties it seemed to suffer a loss of vigour and imagination in the formulation and presentation of policies for any further advance towards social equality, though its last memorable achievement, the 1951 Festival of Britain, intimated how, in more favourable circumstances, a genuine renaissance and social renewal might have come about.

On the world scene the prospects for socialism were further dimmed by the imposition of Stalinist regimes in Eastern Europe, from which only Yugoslavia was able to break away. These totalitarian regimes, which remained dictatorial even after the death of Stalin–although in many cases they gradually became somewhat less oppressive–distorted the image of socialism for four decades, despite the fact that they were consistently criticised and opposed by almost all Western socialists. The relative weakness of the democratic socialist movement as a consequence of these two factors–the revival of capitalism in a more planned, or at least 'managed' form, which resulted in exceptionally high rates of economic growth from the 1950s to the mid-1970s, and the deterrent example of self-styled 'real socialism' in Eastern Europe–made any further extension of social rights much more difficult, although there were some phases of renewed activity such as the great expansion of higher education in the 1960s, and in some circumstances, as in Sweden and Austria where socialist governments were in power over fairly long periods,[2] there was a more continuous development of social welfare policies. To a large extent, moreover, the preoccupation with social welfare, after the immediate post-war changes had been effected and welfare states had been created, in more rudimentary or more elaborate forms, was displaced by an overriding concern with economic growth, resulting partly from the experience of achieved growth in the period of reconstruction, and partly from what Postan (1967) called an 'ideology of growth' which he considered had evolved from earlier debates about full employment. Continuous and rapid growth, achieved by technological innovation, rising productivity and full employment, was now seen as the main foundation of social welfare, assuring to a large part of the population steadily improving conditions of life, and providing, through government expenditure financed by taxation and borrowing, those services and benefits which individuals could not effectively procure for themselves, or which were needed by specific disadvantaged groups in the population. Such changes as the expansion of higher education were themselves closely linked with this concentration on economic growth.

In the period 1950–73, which Maddison (1982, Chapter 6) has described as a 'golden age' of exceptionally high growth rates, the economies of the advanced industrial societies in Western Europe (and in a different form in Japan) tended towards a system of 'managed' capitalism, to which the term 'corporatism'[3] was later applied, characterised by a mixed economy with a limited (and varying) degree of public ownership of productive and service enterprises, and in some cases financial institutions, greatly increased government expenditure as a proportion of the gross national product, and much greater involvement of the state in regulating and to some extent planning the economy. In this system, it was argued, economic and social policy is the product of agreements negotiated between the state, the large capitalist corporations and the trade unions, and some kind of 'class compromise' is reached in order to maintain stability (Offe 1980). Marshall (1972) himself referred to 'a social framework that includes representative government, a mixed economy and a welfare state', and in a later afterthought (1981) he analysed more closely what he called the 'hyphenated society' (e.g. welfare-capitalism) rather than corporatism, and went on to consider its relation to democratic socialism, particularly as this had been expounded by an English socialist, E.F.M. Durbin.

For Durbin, Marshall argued (1981, p. 127), 'the crux of the matter... was the relation between socialism and democracy'. A socialist programme must be 'concerned with the transfer of economic control and the redistribution of real income' (Durbin 1940, p. 290), which was the only road to social justice. 'But the public mind was prone to equate social justice with welfare, which was only part of it, and was likely to press too hard for those purely "ameliorative" measures which affect only the consequences of inequality, not its foundations. The socialist strategy, therefore, must be sure to give a relatively low priority to the social services compared with that given to the more genuinely socialist categories of political action–socialisation of the economy, promotion of prosperity and the redistribution of wealth' (Marshall 1981, pp. 127–8).

This, as Marshall observed, 'goes to the heart of the matter', and he continued (1981, pp. 128–9):

> The wide currency after the war of the term 'welfare state' suggests that there was an urge at that time to find in the concept of 'welfare' a single, unifying axial principle for the new social order. It is not difficult to see why it failed... in this holistic form, it was too vague and nebulous to provide a model for a social system. It expressed a spirit rather than a structure... [and] became quickly associated, or even identified, with that particular, limited sphere of public affairs that we call social policy.

The distinction that Marshall made here was also very clearly formulated by a Hungarian sociologist (Ferge 1979) in the contrast which she drew between 'social policy' and 'societal policy' in her analysis of the changes in Hungarian society, and I shall consider it more fully in relation to the development of citizenship in socialist societies. Marshall, in the passage I have cited, went on to observe that in the system of welfare capitalism and a mixed economy 'the golden calf of democratic socialism had been translated into a troika of sacred cows', and that by the early 1970s the welfare state survived in 'a precarious and somewhat battered condition'. Two decades later it is quite evidently even more battered and precarious, especially in Britain, and numerous studies have been devoted to analysing the 'crisis of the welfare state'.

In the latter part of his essay Marshall (1981, pp. 131–5) considered some of the reasons for what he saw as the declining appeal of the idea of welfare–its 'loss of status'–which he attributed broadly to its loss of identity, emphasising particularly the conflict between the market and welfare as means of satisfying the needs of the population, and especially in dealing with poverty. He summarised his own view as being that democratic freedoms depend to a considerable extent on economic freedom, and that competitive markets make a large contribution to efficiency and economic progress, but on the other hand, that 'the capitalist market economy can be, and generally has been, a cause of much social injustice'; and he concluded that 'the anti-social elements in the capitalist market system which still persist in the mixed economy have to be tackled by action within the economy itself'.

This restates the distinction between socialist and welfare policies, and the dilemma which, as Durbin indicated, is posed for democratic socialist parties, while at the same time it conveys a sense of the direction in which much socialist thought has moved in the post-war period. For it can be said that the European socialist parties (and more recently some communist parties) have in fact become to a large extent 'welfare' parties, whose policies are primarily concerned with, and are seen by a large part of the electorate as being identified with, the promotion of social rights in the narrow sense of providing welfare services in specific areas, rather than with any radical reconstruction of the economic and social system. But this reorientation of thought and policy poses many new problems.

First, the differences between parties in respect of their general policies are attenuated and obscured, and the main issue becomes that of whether there shall be more or less public spending on welfare. This issue is then, however, debated in a context which makes the extension of social rights increasingly difficult, because a sharp distinction is made between the production of wealth, which is conceived as the function of a capitalist market economy, and the distribution of a part of the wealth produced in the form of welfare services. Hence the question can be, and generally is, presented in the form of how much welfare a society can 'afford' in relation to its stock and flow of 'real' wealth provided by mainly private industry. But this is not at all how the issue has been, or should be, formulated in socialist thought, where the fundamental concept is that of the social labour process–that is, productive activity in every sphere, including the provision of welfare services, and involving in advanced economies a massive input of science and technology–and the questions that arise concern the organisation of that process and how its product shall be distributed among various groups in the population. In short, it is not a matter of deducting from some narrowly defined national product that amount which is needed for welfare, but of dividing equitably a national product of which welfare is a major component, and indeed in a broad sense is the sole purpose of the whole labour process. It was clearly in this way that Durbin, like most other socialists, and especially Marxist thinkers, conceived the relation between socialism and welfare, and I shall return to the subject later.

For the present the relation can be illuminated by looking at the experience of the socialist societies in Eastern Europe, especially as it was interpreted by Ferge (1979) in her distinction between 'societal policy' and 'social policy'. Ferge (p. 13) defined these terms in the following way:

The concept of societal policy... is used in a special sense. It encompasses the sphere of *social policy* (the organisation of social services or the redistribution of incomes), but also includes systematic social intervention at all points of the cycle of the reproduction of social life, with the aim of changing the structure of society.

In the following chapters she then traces this process of social reproduction, first describing 'societal policy dealing with the transformation of basic social relations embedded in the social organisation of work', then analysing 'the relations created or modified through distribution and redistribution', and finally considering 'some aspects of social policy in relation to consumption and ways of life in general'. This provides an admirably clear account of the scope of social policy in a socialist perspective, in terms of which the development of citizenship in these societies can be more closely analysed.

In the Soviet Union and other East European countries during the post-war period it is evident that social policy, directed towards the provision of low-cost housing, public transport, leisure facilities, and health care had a high priority, and was complemented by a societal policy which restructured the economy in ways that were intended to achieve rapid industrialisation and economic growth (as they did in the 1950s and 1960s particularly) together with security of employment and in some cases more active participation by workers in the management of production. The citizens of these countries, therefore, acquired a considerable range of important social rights, the value of which is perhaps more clearly recognised since the changes that took place at the end of 1989, but these gains were qualified by a number of adverse factors. First, the level at which welfare services could be provided depended crucially upon economic growth, and from the early 1970s the socialist economies experienced increasing difficulties, exacerbated by the problems of the world economy, and to some extent by an excessively high rate of investment in industry, financed partly by foreign borrowing and often directed to the wrong kind of industry (Bottomore 1990). Secondly, there emerged in all these societies a privileged group—a 'new class' or 'elite', comprising the upper levels of the party and state bureaucracies—which effectively controlled the social labour process and determined the distribution of the product to its own advantage and to the detriment of workers and consumers.

By far the most important factor, however, which ultimately led to the downfall of these regimes, was that the real enlargement of social rights (even though unequally distributed among different groups in the population) was accompanied by a severe restriction of civil and political rights, at its most savage during Stalin's dictatorship but persisting in somewhat less oppressive forms (and notably less oppressive in Yugoslavia from the early 1950s) in the bureaucratic one-party system which followed. Citizenship in these socialist (but far from democratic socialist) societies had, therefore, quite a different character from that which Marshall was considering in relation to Britain and, by implication, other West European societies. Instead of a progression from civil to political rights, and then to a growth of social rights, as Marshall conceived it, these totalitarian state-socialist societies established some important social rights while virtually extinguishing major civil and political rights; though it should be observed that one factor which facilitated this process was that many of the countries involved had no tradition of securely founded civil and political rights, and little experience of democracy, before their 'socialist' transformation.

The ongoing changes in the Soviet Union and Yugoslavia, and the collapse of the other East European regimes, have created an entirely new situation. Civil and political rights have been restored, or are rapidly being restored, although controversy continues, as in the capitalist countries, about the content and limits of some civil rights, and notably the right to own property where this involves ownership of major productive enterprises. Other civil rights, which Marshall listed as being liberty of the person, freedom of speech, thought and faith, and the right to justice, though complex in their details, are uncontested in principle as essential for individual freedom, and their re-establishment is proceeding rapidly. So too is the restoration of political rights–freedom to organise and participate in social movements, associations, and parties of diverse kinds, without authorisation or interference from the state (except where laws which protect basic rights of other citizens are infringed).

The impact of the recent changes on social rights, however, may be very varied. In those countries which are re-establishing a capitalist economy a number of existing social rights are threatened, among them low-cost housing and public transport, and above all security of employment and some degree of participation in the management of enterprises, while in most of the countries the initial measures introduced by the new regimes, together with a general uncertainty about the economic future, have led to a decline in production, falling standards of living, and growing unemployment. How these societies will develop over the next decade is still unclear, but it is evident already from the emergence of new protest movements that existing social rights will be vigorously defended by a large part of the population, and that a major political division over the extent of welfare spending, similar to that in capitalist countries, will reappear, and has indeed done so in several countries. Whether this division will involve an opposition between capitalism and

socialism--whether, that is to say, the revived socialist parties and re-
formed communist parties will connect welfare policy with the maintenance or restoration of public ownership on a significant scale and with
some form of planning, in a conception of 'societal policy' which is
concerned with the social division of the whole product of the labour
process–remains uncertain, just as it is uncertain in the present advanced
capitalist countries.

At all events we may say, as Marshall did, that there is some degree
of conflict between citizenship and the class system of capitalism,
between the satisfaction of needs by welfare services and by the market;
and this conflict has been recognised in various ways by later writers.
Titmuss (1956), in an early essay on the 'societal division of welfare',
raised broad issues concerning welfare and social equality which he
pursued in a later work (1962) on income distribution, where he emphasised the 'class distribution of incomes and wealth' (p. 198), and in
discussing the meaning of poverty came close to a conception of 'societal
policy' that would involve changes in the economic and social structure
in order to achieve greater equality. On the other hand, Robson (1976),
in his study of the achievements and shortcomings of the welfare state,
disputed the view that poverty cannot be abolished in a capitalist society,
citing as an example the case of Sweden (though Sweden has pursued
more 'socialistic' policies than most European countries and has also
experimented recently with means of socialising capital ownership).[4]
Robson concluded his study by saying there there were 'few systematic
views about the nature and aims of the welfare state', and after rejecting
the idea that it is 'just a collection of social services', or 'an instrument
whose main purpose is to abolish poverty', or is 'committed to social and
economic equality as the supreme good' (p. 171), he went on to say that
'welfare is of unlimited scope. It extends to social and economic circumstances, conditions of work, remuneration, the character and scope of
the social services, the quality of the environment, recreational facilities,
and the cultivation of the arts' (p. 174). This suggests more radical
changes in the social structure, and particularly in the class system, than
Robson actually discussed or seemed prepared to consider. His own
emphasis was on what he regarded as essential elements in developing
the welfare state: a high degree of personal freedom, protection of
individual citizens against abuses of power and correlatively, responsible involvement of citizens in the affairs of society, improvement of the
environment, continuous improvement of social services, and an evalu-
ation of the standard of living in terms of a considerable range of criteria,
taking into account not only money incomes, but also such factors as the
quality of the environment, the distribution of wealth, job satisfaction,

health education and housing. This again approaches a conception of a societal policy in which social policy is only one element.

The development of citizenship, and its relationship with social class, is evidently more complex, and as a process more variable, than Marshall's lectures conveyed. In capitalist societies the growth of social rights in the welfare state has not fundamentally transformed the class system, nor have welfare services eliminated poverty in most cases, although the more socialistic countries such as Sweden and Austria have advanced farthest in this respect. In the self-styled 'countries of real socialism' in Eastern Europe some important social rights were established, but equally important civil and political rights were diminished or extinguished, while at the same time new forms of hierarchy and inequality emerged. In capitalist societies too, within the existing class system, new types of stratification developed out of welfare policies, as Marshall, and subsequently other writers, observed. Furthermore, increased state intervention in the economy and in the expansion of welfare services tended to create new hierarchies and a greater centralisation of power, which Robson (1976, pp. 176–7), and from a different perspective, many conservative critics of government bureaucracy, particularly noted.

These are not the only issues, however, which need further consideration. Over the past 40 years problems of citizenship have appeared, and have been widely discussed, in quite new contexts, where the connections with social class are less clear; and in the same period not only have significant changes taken place in the class structure of capitalist societies, but the political conflicts in Eastern Europe have culminated in a rapid transformation of the social structure in the state socialist countries. It is with the new questions posed by these changes that the following two sections of this essay will be concerned.

3. New Questions about Citizenship

Marshall's study of the development of citizenship was made in a particular context. It was concerned with Britain (or indeed more narrowly with England) as a more or less homogeneous society, in the immediate post-war period, although its general conceptions could be more widely applied. Today, however, this context seems no longer adequate. A host of new questions about citizenship have emerged which need to be examined in a broader framework, ideally on a world scale, but at all events with reference to the various types of industrially developed countries, and to the problems of citizenship in societies whose populations are far from being homogeneous.

A useful starting point for such a reconsideration is to be found in the studies by Brubaker (1989, 1992), which examine the problems created by the massive post-war migrations in Europe and North America, against the background of an analysis of the meaning of citizenship in the twentieth century. First, we should note the important distinction made between *formal* and *substantive* citizenship. The former can be defined as 'membership of a nation-state' (Brubaker 1989, p. 3); the latter, in terms of Marshall's conception, as an array of civil, political, and especially social rights, involving also some kind of participation in the business of government. Brubaker (1992, pp. 36–8) then goes on to observe:

> That which constitutes citizenship–the array of rights or the pattern of participation–is not necessarily tied to formal state-membership. Formal citizenship is neither a sufficient nor a necessary condition for substantive citizenship... That it is not a sufficient condition is clear: one can possess formal state-membership yet be excluded (in law or in fact) from certain political, civil, or social rights or from effective participation in the business of rule in a variety of settings... That formal citizenship is not a necessary condition of substantive citizenship is perhaps less evident. Yet while formal citizenship may be required for certain components of substantive citizenship (e.g. voting in national elections), other components... are independent of formal state-membership. Social rights, for example, are accessible to citizens and legally resident non-citizens on virtually identical terms, as is participation in the self-governance of associations, political parties, unions, factory councils, and other institutions...

He then argues that:

> the 'sociologization' of the concept of citizenship in the work of Marshall and Bendix and theorists of participation has indeed been fruitful [but] it has introduced an *endogenous* bias into the study of citizenship. Formal membership of the state has been taken for granted... But the massive immigration of the last quarter-century to Western Europe and North America, leaving in its wake a large population whose formal citizenship is in question, has engendered a new politics of citizenship, centered precisely on the question of membership in the nation-state.

The forms of this new politics of citizenship vary from one country to another, influenced by different conceptions of 'nationhood', and Brubaker (1989, Introduction), in the volume of essays which he edited on immigration and citizenship, makes interesting comparisons between six industrial countries in Europe and North America. First, there is 'a basic difference between nations constituted by immigration and countries in which occasional immigration has been incidental to nation-building. Canada and the United States have a continuous tradition of immigration... and immigration figures prominently in their national myths' (p. 7), But there are also important differences among European countries. In France,

> conceptions of nationhood and citizenship bear the stamp of their revolutionary origin. The nation, in this tradition, has been conceived mainly in relation to the institutional and territorial frame of the state: political unity, not shared culture, has been understood to be its basis (p. 7).

By contrast with this 'universalist, assimilationist, and state-centered' conception, the German conception has been

> particularist, organic, and *Volk*-centered. Because national feeling developed before the nation-state... this German nation... was conceived not as the bearer of universal political values, but as an organic cultural, linguistic, or racial community–as a *Volksgemeinschaft* (p. 8).[5]

Sweden resembles France in that national feeling was attached to political and institutional traditions, and the absence of ethnic or cultural nationalism 'may help explain why Sweden has been able to make citizens of its post-war immigrants with so little fuss or friction' (p. 10). Britain, however, is an exceptional case, where there was (until 1981) no clear conception of citizenship, and 'legal and political status were conceived instead in terms of allegiance', between individual subjects and the monarch; 'ties of allegiance which 'knit together the British Empire, not the British nation'. This absence of a strong identity as a nation–state and of an established national citizenship contributed, Brubaker suggests, 'to the confused and bitter politics of immigration and citizenship during the last quarter-century'. On the other hand, because Britain had not traditionally defined itself as a nation–state, the post-war immigrants have not, for the most part, been considered aliens, and generally have more economic, social, and political rights than elsewhere (pp. 10–11).

Against this background other essays in Brubaker's volume raise broader questions about citizenship, concerning the criteria for access to citizenship, the status of resident non-citizens, and dual citizenship, which I shall examine later in this essay. First, however, it is necessary to consider more fully those new issues that have arisen in respect of the substantive rights of citizens with which Marshall was primarily concerned. Such rights are distinct from the formal rights of citizenship, which are not a sufficient condition for them (see above), although the two sets of rights are plainly interrelated in many respects. The first question to be discussed here is that of gender. Like almost all social scientists at that time Marshall largely ignored gender differences, as even the initial formulation of his theme in terms of whether every man could become a 'gentleman' makes evident. Yet it is obvious that the array of civil, political and social rights whose development Marshall traced was extended to women very much more slowly than to men, in Britain as elsewhere, and that some of these rights are still quite unequally distributed. Civil rights, such as the right to own property, were acquired much later by women, and in Britain, for example, it is only since 1990 that married women have gained the right to independent taxation of their incomes instead of having these regarded as an extension of their husband's earnings. Political rights for women also came much later, during the twentieth century in most countries–in some cases only after 1945–and women still form a small minority in legislative assemblies and in the higher reaches of state administration, though on the other hand they have been increasingly active and prominent in social movements. In the domain of social rights women have usually experienced discrimination, and still do so in most countries, in respect of access to better paid and more prestigious occupations, and prospects for promotion, while social provision in areas which are of particular concern to women, such as day-care nurseries, maternity leave and family planning, has generally been extended less rapidly than have other services.

It should be noted here that particular efforts were made in the socialist countries of Eastern Europe to diminish gender inequality in the sphere of employment, and policies adopted in Hungary (especially those concerning maternity leave and child-care) are discussed in detail by Ferge (1979, pp. 98–112), who also considers some broader aspects of family policy (pp. 211–22). But as Ferge observes, traditionally ingrained attitudes and ideas perpetuate gender inequality, notably in the family, where domestic labour is disproportionately performed by women even though both spouses are working, in socialist as well as capitalist countries;[6] and such attitudes can only be influenced very gradually by policies aimed at extending and equalising social rights. Hence the new feminist movements which developed after the war, and especially rapidly in the 1960s, have been concerned not only with civil, political, and social rights as generally understood, but also with the gender stereotypes which profoundly affect the personal and family life of women.[7] Any discussion of citizenship today is obliged, therefore, to consider specifically the social position of women–whether they are still, in many countries, and in certain respects (if decreasingly), 'second-class citizens'–and this poses new questions about the scope and content of social rights.

A second issue that raises similar questions is that of ethnic or ethno-cultural diversity, which has increased in many countries as a result of large-scale post-war immigration. This has created problems both of formal and substantive citizenship, and policies with regard to the former have varied considerably between countries–for example, between Germany, France, and Britain–although there has been a general tendency in the past decade to restrict immigration and access to citizenship. Even where formal citizenship exists, however, the substantive rights of citizenship may not be acquired in practice, or only in an unequal degree, by particular ethnic groups. The civil rights movement of black (Afro-)Americans in the 1960s was a dramatic instance of protest against the effective denial of civil, political, and social rights to a major ethnic group in American society; and other ethnic groups have likewise campaigned, and continue to campaign, against discrimination, particularly in the sphere of social rights, in the USA and other countries. If social rights are interpreted broadly to include access to education, health care, employment, and adequate housing (as is certainly implied in many conceptions of the post-war welfare state), and in addition provision for the special needs of particular groups (for example, working mothers), then it is evident that some of these rights are still very unequally distributed, not only between men and women, but also between groups defined by ethnic and/or cultural characteristics, in many of the countries of welfare capitalism.

Ethnic and cultural differences within nation-states have also posed other problems of citizenship where particular groups–for example in the province of Quebec in Canada, in the Basque country in Spain, in Northern Ireland, and increasingly in Eastern Europe following the collapse of the state-socialist regimes–have initiated movements to achieve a more distinct separate nationhood, in the form of complete independence, or at the least of much greater regional autonomy, or in some cases by adhesion to, or incorporation into, another nation-state. Some of these movements in effect raise the question of a kind of dual citizenship, which is also raised in a different way by such developments towards supra-national political systems as the European Community, where a 'European' citizenship seems to be evolving, already expressed in an embryonic body of rights upheld by the European Court and the Commission on Human Rights, and in the proposals by the European Parliament for a new 'social charter'.

These complexities of modern citizenship, and their implications for conceptions of nationhood and the nation-state, will be considered more fully later. Meanwhile, there are other aspects of the substantive rights of citizens within existing nation-states to be discussed, and in particular the consequences of poverty for such rights. Tawney (1952) wrote of 'gross and crushing disabilities' which placed those experiencing them 'at a permanent disadvantage' (see above, p. 56), and Marshall (p. 33

above) conceived the development of citizenship as 'a general enrichment of the concrete substance of civilised life', to be achieved by
reducing risk and insecurity, and equalising the conditions of the more
and the less fortunate. Undoubtedly, in the 1940s and 1950s, one of the
principal aims of the welfare state was seen as the eradication of poverty,
especially by eliminating the large-scale and long-term unemployment
which was one of its major causes, but in any case countering the effects
of such unemployment as did occur by social security payments on as
generous a scale as possible. Initially these policies were fairly effective
and social conditions improved considerably compared with the 1930s,
but over the past two decades, and particularly in the 1980s, poverty has
increased again in most West European countries, although Sweden and
Austria are notable exceptions to the general trend. Above all, poverty
has increased in Britain, where economic decline, changes in fiscal
policy, large-scale unemployment, and diminishing social expenditure
have combined to re-create massive inequalities of wealth and income,
and a large category of very poor, predominantly working-class citizens.

In the USA and Britain the term 'underclass' has come to be widely
used to describe this category, but as Lister (1990, pp. 24–6) points out,
there is an ideological element involved in applying this stigmatising
label, which tends to define the poor in moral rather than economic
terms, and indeed to revive nineteenth-century conceptions of the poor
as being responsible for their own poverty. There is also much disagree-
ment about how large this so-called 'underclass' is in Britain, with
estimates ranging from 5 per cent to 30 per cent of the population, but
there can be no doubt at any rate that the extent of poverty has greatly
increased during the past decade, and that poverty has substantial effects
on the quality of citizenship for those afflicted by it.

Lister begins her study by quoting Marshall's definition of citizenship
as 'a status bestowed on those who are full members of a community.
All who possess the status are equal with respect to the rights and duties
with which the status is endowed' (p. 18 above), and goes on to consider
the debate about citizenship during the past decade, in which the ideas
of the New Right have been directed against what is called the 'dependency culture'–that is to say, the body of social rights established by the
community as a whole–and in favour of an 'enterprise culture' in which
private individuals secure their own welfare by their own efforts, and
the role of the state (or of private charity) is limited to providing help to
those who, for one reason or another, are unable to help themselves.
The dominance of this ideology, now embodied in social policies, has
gradually undermined social rights as an attribute of citizenship, placing
all the emphasis on privatised activities (private health care and educa-

tion, privatised municipal services, the introduction of commercial activities into public services of all kinds), and treating the poor generally as recipients of charity who are effectively regarded as second-class citizens. It is not only the social rights of the poor which are affected however, and Lister (pp. 32–40) points to the limitation of civil rights as a result of the inability of many poor citizens to assert their rights through the legal process, and in particular the deficiencies of the legal aid and advice system, as compared with its initial promise which Marshall (pp. 29–31 above) saw as an important step towards equalising civil rights. Lister (pp. 41–6) also notes the various ways in which the poor tend to lose political rights and to become politically 'marginalised', and she rightly draws attention to the influence of economic and social factors in this process.

But the deterioration of the substantive rights of citizenship–civil, political and social–in Britain is due primarily to recent government policies, facilitated by the peculiarities of the British political and electoral system, and it is somewhat exceptional in Western Europe as a whole. In several European countries, to be sure, there have been constraints on the development of the welfare state and the growth of public expenditure that it entails, largely in response to the slowing down of economic growth, but nowhere else has the conception of social rights in particular been rejected in such a thoroughgoing way. In Britain, as Marshall (1981) observed, the welfare state survived at the end of the 1970s in a 'precarious and somewhat battered condition', and by the beginning of the 1990s this was evidently still more the case. In most of Western Europe, however, the welfare system has weathered the economic recession and the doctrines of the New Right rather more successfully, and the countries of the European Community (with the exception of Britain) have indeed signalled their desire to extend social rights through the proposals for a 'social charter'. To a surprising degree already, some of the rights of British citizens are now sustained by European institutions such as the European Court and the Commission on Human Rights; and political rights may well be extended through the influence of the other member countries of the European Community that have systems of proportional representation, now introduced into the voting procedure for the European Parliament. In this sphere, membership of the EC has stimulated a growing movement in Britain (Charter 88) for radical democratic reform of the political system, and it seems that the British may before long finally become citizens in a modern sense rather than subjects of the Crown'.

In the light of the discussion so far we can now consider the ways in which citizenship has developed over the past four decades, and the problems that have emerged for the kind of continuous enlargement of citizens' rights that Marshall envisaged. As I have noted, questions of formal citizenship (that is, membership of a nation-state) have assumed greater importance, for several reasons: (i) the large post-war immigration into some countries of foreign workers, who may be denied citizenship even though long resident (as is the case with the so-called 'guest-workers' in Germany); (ii) a growing 'internationalisation' of employment, especially in the European Community, which results from the internationalisation of economic activities and creates significant groups of legally resident aliens; and (iii) arising out of these processes more general issues concerning the relation between residence and citizenship, and the extent to which the nation-state should still be regarded as the sole, or principal, locus of citizenship in its substantive sense. Here, the important question arises of whether the rights of citizens should be conceived rather as the human rights of all individuals who are settled members of a community, regardless of their formal membership of a nation-state, and I shall discuss this larger issue at the end of this essay.

The development of substantive citizenship itself has followed a more uneven and variable course than was expected, and hoped for, by Marshall and other writers 40 years ago. The post-war welfare state then seemed to hold out the promise of more equal civil and political rights, and a substantial expansion of social rights which would gradually establish greater economic and social equality. In this sense the idea of citizenship did express a 'principle of equality', but this conflicted with the inequality embodied in the capitalist economic system and the class structure; and the outcome of the contest between the two depended not only on the extension of welfare in the narrower sense of the social services, health care, education, or even full employment, but on changes in property ownership, economic control and the distribution of real income, as Marshall (1981) recognised in his discussion of Durbin's exposition of democratic socialism (see above, pp. 59–61). In the 1950s and 1960s, in most of the West European countries, there was some progress towards greater equality in both these spheres; changes in the distribution of wealth and income, and in economic control through various forms of 'mixed economy', as well as expansion and improvement in the provision of welfare, facilitated by exceptionally high rates of economic growth.

But from the mid-1970s, as economic growth rates declined, the expansion of welfare and social rights was checked. Rising unemployment and ageing populations (and in some countries increased military expenditure) made greater demands on the state budget, while at the same time the mixed economy appeared to be functioning less successfully. Out of these conditions grew the new political doctrines and movements, most prominent in Britain and the USA, which advocated (and in those two countries particularly, implemented as far as possible) policies of retrenchment in government expenditure and a return to *laissez-faire* capitalism. As a result, in Britain notably, and to some extent elsewhere, inequality has increased again, and the capitalist market economy has become dominant over the welfare state. We need, therefore, to reconsider, in the light of post-war experience, what is the relationship between citizenship and social class, and how, in varying circumstances and in different countries, it may fluctuate.

4. Changing Classes, Changing Doctrines

The development of substantive citizenship as a growing body of civil, political, and social rights needs to be explained as well as described, and it is not enough to conceive this process in abstract, teleological terms as one that is somehow immanent in the rise of modern capitalism. Specific social groups were involved in the struggles to extend or restrict such rights, and in these conflicts social classes have played a major part. Marshall recognised that an element of conflict existed, but he expressed it as a clash between opposing principles rather than between classes, and his discussion of class was primarily concerned, as he said, with the impact of citizenship on social class, not with the ways in which the historical development of classes had itself generated new conceptions of citizenship and movements to expand the rights of citizens.

But the impact of class on citizenship is unmistakable. Civil rights, and to some extent political rights, were gained by the burgesses of medieval towns in opposition to the feudal aristocracy, and subsequently on a more extensive, national scale by the bourgeoisie in the early stages of development of industrial capitalism. In the nineteenth century the struggle to extend political rights was carried on mainly by the working class movement, in the revolutions of 1848, the Chartist movement, and the later campaigns for universal suffrage which had a prominent place in the activities of the rapidly growing socialist parties in Europe. These struggles continued into' the twentieth century and broadened into campaigns for social rights, instigated primarily by trade unions and socialist parties, and forming part of a more general movement towards socialism. The post-war welfare state in Western Europe was largely the outcome of these class-based actions, and in the period from the late 1940s to the early 1970s a kind of equilibrium seemed to have been attained, in the form of 'welfare capitalism' and a 'mixed economy', which Schumpeter (1949) characterised as a possible 'halfway house' on the march into socialism, and later social scientists described as neo-capitalism, organised capitalism or corporatism (Panitch 1977). In this system the interventionist state had a crucial role in negotiating agreements with large capital and organised labour, whereby a 'class compromise' could be reached (Offe 1980).

This compromise, and a degree of underlying consensus about the role of the state in the welfare-capitalist society, depended on the relative strength and the political orientations of different classes, and also to a large extent on the exceptionally high rates of economic growth in the period from the end of the war to the early 1970s. Economic growth and the enlargement of social rights in turn had an important effect on the class structure, as Marshall envisaged in his discussion of the impact of citizenship on social class. In the first place, the antecedent extension of political rights in the course of the twentieth century—itself, as I have argued, the outcome of class actions—had made possible the rapid growth of working-class parties in Western Europe (particularly marked after 1945) in terms of both membership and electoral support in most countries; and this was the crucial factor in the post-war development of social rights within what remained predominantly capitalist economies. At the same time working-class parties (mainly socialist or social democratic) had a conception of citizenship and social rights going considerably beyond what is ordinarily seen as the provision of welfare services. This embodied ideas of radical educational reform, the elimination of poverty, full employment as a major objective, economic democracy, which would involve the socialisation of basic, large-scale industrial, financial and service enterprises, and a general enhancement of the economic role of the state, including national planning in various forms. All this clearly pointed beyond a welfare state towards a more socialist form of society, as was recognised from different points of view in such writings as those of Schumpeter and Durbin, and expressed in the policies of the first post-war Labour government in Britain.

The policies and actions of socialist parties, in some cases as the government, in other cases an an influential partner in coalitions or as a powerful opposition, did in fact result in an extension of public ownership and economic planning in Western Europe, though in different degrees in individual countries; and the introduction of macro-economic planning in particular, it may be argued (Bottomore 1990, Chapter 3), was an important factor in the sustained economic growth of what Maddison (1982, p. 96) called the 'golden age' from 1950 to 1973. These changes, however, produced significant changes in the class structure and in the social and political outlook of different classes. First, post-war economic development, in which rapid technological innovation was a prominent feature, and the expansion of welfare rights (and hence the range of activities of government) steadily diminished the numbers of the manual working class and increased the numbers of those employed in white-collar, service occupations which ranged from clerical work to professional and technical activities in both private and public enterprises and in the extensive social services.[8] In the advanced industrial countries the manual working class now constitutes only half or less of the occupied population.

At the same time the economic situation of the working class changed substantially as a result of economic growth, full employment (until the early 1970s), the expansion of welfare services, and increased opportunities for social mobility determined mainly by the changing occupational structure, but also by somewhat improved access to education. Its social situation, compared with the nineteenth century and the earlier part of the twentieth century, also changed through the acquisition of important civil, political and social rights; that is to say, as a result of the growth of citizenship in Marshall's sense, which produced a condition very far removed from Marx's depiction of it in the 1840s as that of 'a class *in* civil society which is not a class *of* civil society', a class which experienced a '*total loss* of humanity' (Marx 1844). This transformation of the economic and social position of workers in the second half of the twentieth century gave rise, from the late 1950s, to much study and discussion of such phenomena as the 'affluent worker', the 'embourgeoisement' of the working class, and the emergence of a new type of 'middle-class society'. Some of the claims made about the degree to which such fundamental changes had occurred, or were occurring, were undoubtedly exaggerated, as were the conclusions drawn from them. They were critically examined, in the case of Britain, in a series of studies summarised in Goldthorpe et al. (1969), where the authors concluded that when three major aspects of the everyday lives of affluent workers – work, patterns of sociability, aspirations and social perspectives – are examined, the findings show that 'there remain important areas of common social experience which are still fairly distinctively working class', and that the evidence 'is sufficient to show how the thesis [of embourgeoisement] can in fact break down fairly decisively at any one of several points' (p. 157). Other criticisms of the thesis were made by those who pointed to the emergence of a 'new working class' of more affluent, skilled and technically qualified workers who still gave their allegiance to the traditional working class parties (Mallet 1975), and on the other side by those who drew attention to a process of 'proletarianisation' of some sections of the middle class (Renner 1953, Braverman 1974).[9]

At all events it is evident at the present time that the distinction between working class and middle class persists in the capitalist industrial countries (and is now reappearing in the former state socialist societies of Eastern Europe), expressed in the divergent conceptions of social welfare and of the rights of citizenship that are expressed in the programmes and policies of rival, largely class-based parties. These societies can only be regarded as 'middle class' in the limited sense that the middle class, broadly defined, now forms a much larger part of the population; and even then such a conception requires that we should ignore the existence of a wealthy upper class, comprising the owners of large capital, which continues to dominate the economy and many other areas of social life, as well as the very great differentiation within the middle class itself in terms of property ownership, level of income, education and style of life. Nevertheless, the expansion of the middle class as a whole, in conjunction with economic growth and the extension of welfare services, did bring about significant changes in social and political attitudes. By the early 1970s, as I noted earlier, it was widely held that some kind of equilibrium and a broad consensus of opinion had been established in the West European societies on the basis of a welfare state or welfare society, a mixed economy, and a democratic political system. This view was reflected in the programmes of most political parties, and especially the socialist parties, which concentrated their attention increasingly on welfare policies rather than on such longer-term, traditional socialist aims as the extension of public ownership and the achievement of a more fundamental equality in the economic and social condition of all citizens, which used to be described as a 'classless' society.

How far this reorientation of party politics (which was more pronounced in some countries than in others) corresponded with a distinct change in social attitudes within particular classes is a matter of contention. The radical upheavals of the late 1960s indicated the limits of the consensus and the existence of widespread dissatisfaction in some parts of society (though not very prominently in the working class) with the existing hierarchical system; and while the immediate outcome of these events was a strengthening of conservative forces, their effects in the longer term–manifested, for example, in the growth of the women's movement, of green parties, and of the democratic opposition in Eastern Europe–have been more radical. Most attention has been given, however, to the question of changes in working-class attitudes. In some countries during the 1970s and 1980s, and most clearly in Britain, an increasing number of workers, particularly those who were in more highly paid skilled occupations, did transfer their allegiance from socialist parties to liberal or conservative parties, and this undoubtedly reflected in some way a change in the character of their principal economic and social concerns. Full employment, economic growth and an extensive welfare system had brought greater prosperity for a majority of the population, and along with this a preoccupation with individual or family standards of living and an emphasis on private consumption, aided by a rapid expansion of consumer credit. Hence the more prosperous workers, as well as a considerable part of the middle class, became as much or more concerned about inflation, interest rates and levels of personal taxation as about the expansion of the welfare state or the extension of public ownership, which seemed to have less significance for individual well-being. The general nature of this change might be depicted, as by Goldthorpe and Lockwood (1963)–although they were subsequently more critical of the idea of 'embourgeoisement' (see above, p. 75)–as the emergence of 'a distinctive view of society which diverges both from the radical individualism of the old middle class and from the comprehensive collectivism of the old working class'. In this view collectivism is accepted as a means ('instrumental collectivism'), but not as an end, the latter being conceived in more individualistic or family-centred terms, as involving the family's standard of living, the prospects for occupational advancement and the educational and career opportunities for children.

A change of this kind from a more collectivist to a more individualistic social outlook, did probably begin to manifest itself in the late 1950s and through the 1960s,[10] but we should not exaggerate either its novelty, its extent, its universality across countries or its durability. With the development of capitalism, and especially the growth of large corporations, the desire for individual advancement in the occupational hierarchy had already become very powerful early in this century, as Hilferding (1910, p. 347), among others, had noted, but such individualistic aspirations were greatly strengthened by the exceptional economic growth after the Second World War. Yet the extent to which individual and family-centred aims came to prevail was restrained in all the West European countries by a continuing strong attachment of working-class organisations (trade unions and political parties) to the collectivist, and in varying degrees egalitarian, aims that were symbolised above all by the welfare state, and to a lesser degree by public ownership. Furthermore, in those countries where socialist parties were particularly strong–in the Scandinavian countries and especially Sweden, in Austria and West Germany, and in France after 1981–there was little diminution in the support for collectivist ends, and in continental Western Europe as a whole there has been no very marked movement away from the established pattern of welfare provision and public ownership.[11] The virulent attack on the 'dependency culture' and the massive privatisation of public assets which characterised the outlook and policies of the government in Britain during the 1980s, were therefore quite exceptional.

Nevertheless, it may reasonably be argued that in most countries, by the late 1960s, there was no very strong or widespread desire among large sections of the working class, or in those sections of the middle class which had supported and benefited from the welfare state, to extend significantly either the scope of welfare provision or more particularly public ownership. The existing level of public services, including health and education, though capable of steady improvement, seemed to many people adequate, and the growing prosperity of a large part of the population had diverted attention, as I have noted, from collective provision to the concerns of individuals as consumers.

Since the mid-1970s, however, several factors have brought about a radical change in this situation. Ageing populations entailed higher levels of public spending on pensions and on health services, and this financial pressure on the welfare state was increased by economic recession and a general slackening of economic growth, accompanied by rising unemployment which made fresh demands on public expenditure. At the same time, expectations concerning the quality of public services continued to rise. In Britain, which had experienced since the 1950s growth rates lower than those of many other West European countries (or of Japan and the USA), a decline in manufacturing, and recurrent economic crises, the problems were more acute than elsewhere, and it is hardly surprising that by the end of the 1970s, the British welfare state should have been in a particularly debilitated condition, while the general economic situation provoked sharp fluctuations in political attitudes. By the end of the 1980s, however, the 'new economic policy' pursued for a decade had left the British economy in a still more parlous condition and the welfare state facing a still more uncertain future, in stark contrast with most other West European countries, including other member states of the European Community, which had coped more successfully with the economic recession—to some extent by means of effective economic planning—while retaining a 'mixed' economy of private and public ownership (and in some cases extending the latter), and in several countries even expanding welfare services.

Britain, during the past decade, has pursued idiosyncratic economic and social policies which contrast strongly with those of other European countries and have a greater affinity (also in respect of the problems they have engendered) with the policies of the USA in the same period. Of course, all the industrial societies had to face the difficulties created by recession and more sluggish economic growth from the mid-1970s, but most of the West European countries responded in a different way, maintaining more successfully their welfare systems, their various forms of mixed economy, and an important element of central planning. Hence, in considering the recent development of social rights it is essential to look beyond the case of Britain to the wider, especially European, context. Rydén and Bergström (1982), for example, note that in spite of the harsher economic conditions of the 1970s Sweden continued its policies of democratisation of working life and expansion of the public sector, emphasising the improvement of the environment, increased leisure, and greater scope for making the decisions that affect one's life;[12] and they conclude that 'Swedish society and the Swedish economy–the welfare state–have proved enormously strong against the instability and crises of the 1970s' (p. 8). Similarly, in Austria, the predominantly socialist governments since 1970 have not only maintained the welfare system but have extended social welfare programmes and progressively increased the participation of workers in the management of industry.

The experience of both countries shows how it is possible, even in more difficult conditions, to sustain a high level of material prosperity, low unemployment and low inflation, and at the same time to promote policies which extend the social rights of citizens. Their example has also had a significant influence elsewhere; for example, French governments since 1981, except for a short interlude of bi-partisan compromise, embarked on policies of extending public ownership, as well as increasing public expenditure on welfare services and on the social infrastructure (notably railways). Other European countries, while they have not been so strongly committed to extending social welfare, have for the most part maintained the existing levels of welfare expenditure, and unlike Britain they have not given an overriding priority to reducing public expenditure, privatising public assets, and encouraging the development of an unfettered market economy. The social and political orientation of most of the West European countries can be inferred to some extent from the policies of the European Community. In the European Parliament socialist parties and allied groups now form a majority, and their influence will be a significant factor in shaping the new European 'social charter', which envisages not only a progressive improvement of welfare rights but also an extension of industrial democracy through increased representation of workers in the management of industry. That, together with the influence of countries such as Sweden and Austria which are not at present members of the EC–though likely to join in the course of the 1990s–will probably bring about an enlargement of social rights throughout Europe, which will also affect conditions in Eastern Europe, and in the longer term raise questions about social rights in the Third World. At the same time these developments are bound to provoke a reconsideration of what social rights *are*, and how far they can be defined in terms of citizenship, and I shall discuss this issue more fully in the following section of this essay.

What is clear at this point is that conceptions of rights, welfare and citizenship vary significantly across the political spectrum. The compromise or consensus of the 1950s and 1960s has largely broken down, and in Britain no longer exists at all, so that there is now more evidently a sharp division between left and right, between the contending principles of equality and inequality which Marshall regarded as being implicit in the relation between citizenship and capitalism. Conservative governments, especially where they have been influenced by the doctrines of the New Right,[13] are primarily concerned to limit, or reduce, public spending (except, in some cases, in the military sphere), and to enhance the role of private enterprise and markets. Socialist governments, on the other hand, are more inclined to maintain, and so far as possible increase, public spending (especially on education, health, and other welfare services); to regulate market relations by various means, including some degree of economic planning; to maintain a substantial element of public ownership (or to increase it) in a mixed economy, and more generally to encourage greater participation by workers in management. In addition, they aim to promote greater economic equality by fiscal and other measures.[14] Some part of these socialist policies (for example, welfare expenditure in some areas, and a mixed economy so long as the public sector is not too large) may also be supported by liberal and centre parties, which have sometimes been influential in coalition governments.

It remains the case, however, that governments of all political complexions have faced during the past two decades some general problems, such as I mentioned earlier, arising from ageing populations, slower economic growth, and the accompanying rise in unemployment, in maintaining or improving the level of welfare services. Here it should also be noted that lower rates of economic growth are not to be regarded simply as a temporary effect of various external shocks, but need to be considered in a much broader context which takes account of the environmental consequences of high growth rates. The 'growth-addiction' of the post-war period in the industrial and industrialising countries now seems more questionable,[15] and comparisons of aggregate growth rates, without regard to what is growing or what the ecological effects may be, no longer seem at all satisfactory as a measure of the level of welfare, in its broadest sense, in different countries. Looked at more closely indeed these general problems also intimate the existence of other important differences between conservative and socialist parties in their approach to welfare policies. Thus, the changing age structure of the population in the industrial societies, as well as the extension of the period of formal education, call for new reflection on the way in which the social product is divided between different age categories, not simply for palliative measures to deal with hardship among young people or the elderly; and such new conceptions of the division of social welfare are more likely to come from socialist parties. Similarly, low growth rates, which may indeed be desirable in some areas as I have suggested, raise questions particularly about where, and to what extent, growth should be stimulated–for example, in the provision of low-cost housing and improved health care–and this involves a degree of economic planning going beyond what is generally acceptable to conservative parties. The unemployment which is an outcome of economic recession in the traditional areas of capitalist growth does not only add considerably, and wastefully, to public expenditure, but also has a generally demoralising effect on the substantial part of the population which is exposed to it, as well as effectively diminishing their rights as citizens (see above, p. 71). Here the contrast between very right-wing conservative governments, as in Britain, and such socialist governments as those in Sweden and Austria, in the nature and effectiveness of their policies to combat unemployment, is striking.

We have still to consider, however, a further aspect of the development of social rights, which is alluded to by Rydén and Bergström (1982; see above p. 79) when they refer to the sense of alienation experienced by the individual confronting large bureaucracies. This, as they make clear, does not arise only from the existence of public bureaucracies, but as Schumpeter also argued (1942, p. 206), from the general bureaucratisation of life in modern industrial societies, which are increasingly dominated, in almost every sphere, by very large, bureaucratically managed organisations. Nevertheless, it is probably in relation to public bureaucracies that individuals have felt most frustrated, as was most evident in the state socialist countries of Eastern Europe, though here the major resentment was directed specifically against the political dictatorship of communist parties and rule by party officials. In Western Europe the frustrations were experienced more diffusely, and in different ways by particular groups in the population, as limitations on personal freedom, or as problems of the inadequacy or inefficiency of public services; and in Britain especially such sentiments no doubt had some effect in bringing about a change towards a more individualistic attitude, although dissatisfaction with the poor performance of the economy was a more potent factor, and in the last few years there has been a resurgence of support for increased spending on social welfare.

In any advanced welfare system, however, there are bound to be problems in attaining a balance between efficient administration and concern for the individual as a consumer of public services, between the restrictions necessarily imposed by welfare policies and the liberty of the individual. The achievement of such a balance, which is never likely to reach a state of perfection, may be helped by a greater involvement of consumer groups, and of charitable organisations and mutual aid groups, in the operation of the welfare services, as is discussed in the most recent edition of Marshall's *Social Policy* (completed by A.M. Rees, 1985, Chapter 13). Here, as elsewhere, some mixture of public and private endeavour (the latter, in the form of voluntary associations, being itself an expression of citizenship) may be valuable, even though the foundation and main structure of the welfare system is constituted essentially by publicly provided services.

At work, in the process of production, the individual is faced with either private or public bureaucracies, and individual welfare in this sphere depends very clearly upon the extent of social rights. Health and safety regulations, a statutory minimum wage, the protection given by independent trade unions, are necessary elements in this body of rights, but they need to be complemented by other rights which would give workers more control over the labour process itself, through greater participation in the management of enterprises. This kind of extension of social rights has been undertaken in various forms–in the system of self-management in Yugoslavia, and in other ways, which may be more or less comprehensive, in countries such as Austria, Germany and Sweden–and it is envisaged on a wider scale in the European Community's proposals for a social charter.

It may well be, therefore, that after 1992, with the creation of a single market in the European Community, the eventual accession of new members, and a continuing process of unification, there will be a substantial extension of social rights, and to some extent of civil and political rights, in a direction which has been advocated particularly by socialist parties. But any such extension will need to pay more attention to eradicating those specific inequalities which arise from differences of gender or ethno-cultural origins, and will also confront larger issues concerning the definition and scope of social rights, their implications for the economic structure and the class system, and the relation between social rights in the advanced industrial countries and the rights of individuals elsewhere in the world, especially in the poorest countries.

It is to those broader questions that I shall now turn.

5. A Kind of Conclusion

In this essay I have moved some way beyond the themes which Marshall discussed in 1949. The new questions that are raised here concern the relation between formal and substantive citizenship; the connection between rights and citizenship; the diverse and conflicting conceptions of the nature and extent of social rights; the role of classes, and other social groups, in the development of such rights; the tensions between a capitalist market economy and a welfare state, arising from their different aims and outcomes; and the variations of citizenship, in principle and practice, between nations. These questions now need to be more closely considered.

The growing interest in formal citizenship–that is, membership of a nation-state–has been provoked to a large extent by the scale of post-war migration, actual and potential, to the advanced industrial countries. Citizenship, in its formal, legal sense, is clearly a major factor affecting the attribution of rights, even though it is neither a necessary nor a sufficient condition for the effective possession or exercise of various rights (see above p. 66); and the post-war migrations, especially of workers from poorer countries during the period of rapid economic growth up to the early 1970s, led in due course to more stringent definitions of eligibility for citizenship in some industrial countries, and to stricter immigration controls in most of them. From these conditions there has emerged a new debate about formal citizenship, as well as organisations campaigning for more liberal policies in the conferment of citizenship on long-term residents (and on the other side nationalist, not to say xenophobic, movements which aim to exclude or expel foreign workers); and the debate has raised important issues concerning the nature of citizenship in the modern world, and the relationship between residence and citizenship.

Several contributors to Brubaker's (1989) volume discuss various aspects of these questions. Thus Carens (p. 31) argues that 'those allowed to reside and work in a nation should be granted the right to become citizens following a moderate passage of time and some reasonable formalities', basing his argument on 'principles that are implicit in the institutions and practices of liberal democratic societies'. Schuck, however, writing from a similar standpoint, suggests that in the USA changes in recent decades 'have reduced almost to the vanishing point the marginal value of citizenship as compared to resident alien status' (p. 52), and he notes that 'a large number of aliens who are eligible to naturalise fail to do so', one reason for this probably being 'many aliens' continuing hope to return to their native lands to live' (p. 57). In this context Hammar raises the question of dual citizenship, pointing out that in spite of international efforts to limit it 'the number of persons holding more than one citizenship has increased substantially in recent decades and will probably continue to increase' (p. 81). He also observes that there is a large and growing group of 'privileged non citizens', especially in continental Europe, for whom he suggests using the term 'denizens', who have the right to settle in the country, work there, receive social benefits, and even in some circumstances to vote (pp. 83–4).

Dual citizenship raises important political issues in relation to the nation-state and nationality, especially concerning 'dual loyalties', and Hamman goes on to examine some of the problems that emerge, both for states and for individuals, from the reality that 'the formally simple notion of citizenship is in fact a very complex one' (p. 86). The question of dual citizenship is likely to become still more important in Europe, in another sense, as the European Community moves towards closer economic and political union. In effect, citizens of the EC countries will increasingly have a kind of dual citizenship, already existing to some extent, in the EC and their own nation. But this also raises questions about the situation of 'denizens' in the future Community. The creation, from 1992, of a 'Europe without frontiers' will establish freedom of movement within the EC for those who are formally citizens of a member country, not for 'denizens' who are outside this category, and some observers fear that the outcome may be a 'Fortress Europe' with more severe restrictions on entry and immigration for non-citizens.

More generally, the discussions of dual citizenship raise major questions about the connection between citizenship, residence, and the rights of the individual. These rights are already to a considerable extent dissociated from formal citizenship, as Schuck has noted in the case of the USA, and as will be the case (with the qualifications I have indicated) in the EC. Increasingly, civil and social rights, and with some limitations political rights, are granted to all those who live and work, or are retired, in a particular country, regardless of their national citizenship. On the other side, the significance of formal citizenship is to be found mainly in the desire of at any rate a substantial proportion of the population in nation-states to maintain a distinct and separate identity which is the product of a historical tradition, long-established institutions, and a national culture; and the importance of such formal citizenship can be seen not only in the case of existing nation-states, but also in the various movements of 'nations within nation-states' for greater autonomy or complete independence. Nevertheless, this kind of attachment to a particular nation is somewhat diminished by the growth of dual citizenship, and in Europe it may be further reduced by the process of integration in the EC, even though in Eastern Europe at the present time there is an upsurge of nationalist and separatist movements. 16

From this discussion it will be apparent that formal citizenship and substantive citizenship raise issues of very different kinds; in one case concerning national identity and the historical role of nation-states as the pre-eminent modern form of organisation of a political community, in the other concerning the rights, and particularly the social rights, of individuals living in a community. We should therefore go on to consider whether the idea of citizenship now provides the most useful conceptual framework within which to examine the development of individual rights. The alternative would be to conceive a body of human rights which each individual should possess in any community in which he or she lives and/or works, regardless of national origins and formal citizenship. This body of rights will necessarily vary between different groups of countries, depending to a considerable extent, especially in the case of social rights, upon the level of economic and social development, and I shall confine my discussion largely to the advanced industrial societies.

In these countries themselves, however, rights are still developing, and while it is illuminating in many respects to conceive, as Marshall did, of a progression from civil to political and then to social rights, this tends to obscure the fact that civil and political rights have not been established once and for all, in some near-perfect form, as the basis from which social rights can develop, but are also capable of further extension. Civil rights, including personal liberty, freedom of thought and speech, the right to own property, and access to justice through the courts, are more or less well established, in various forms, in the industrial countries, but many questions concerning them are still hotly debated: such as whether they should be embodied in a bill of rights, and in legislation concerning freedom of information; to what extent the ownership and use of property (especially productive property) should be regulated; what measures are needed to ensure that access to justice is not only in principle, but effectively, equal for all members of the community, whatever their economic and social circumstances.

The industrial countries are, in different ways, political democracies, but here too many controversial issues arise concerning how democratic they are; how far their political institutions and electoral systems allow the effective expression of diverse social and political attitudes, whether government should be more 'open' and less elitist, and whether democracy should be extended more widely, especially in the economic sphere, in order to encourage and facilitate more active participation in decision-making at all levels of social life.[17] It should also be taken into account in considering the idea of a general progression of rights that in the state-socialist societies of Eastern Europe, until the recent changes, important social rights were established while civil and political rights were severely curtailed. Following the collapse of the communist regimes at the end of 1989, and the cumulative reforms in the Soviet Union, basic civil rights, and political democracy in the form of multi-party systems and free elections, have been restored or created for the first time; but this achievement brings these societies to the point where wider issues of the effective exercise of civil and political rights become matters of controversy. Already in some countries social movements which played a leading role in bringing about the changes have been marginalised, while new nationalist, as well as class movements and parties have emerged. At the same time important social rights, as they were conceived in the social policies of the previous regimes (full employment, low-cost housing and public transport, maternity leave and child care facilities) are either under threat or already being whittled away.

In all the industrial countries indeed, social rights are those which are most fiercely debated, not only with regard to the existing provision for education, health care, pensions, unemployment benefits and other kinds of social assistance in welfare states that differ in their level of development, but in respect of the scope of social rights in principle, and the place they should occupy in the social and societal[18] policies of an advanced industrial country. Do social rights include such things as adequate housing, provided if necessary by public authorities, employment, some degree of participation by employees in the management of enterprises, and protection against discrimination on grounds of ethnic origin or gender? These issues clearly divide political parties of the left and right, along lines which I indicated earlier, but they also involve social movements and organisations concerned with the rights of particular groups in the population: women, pensioners, the very poor, the homeless, the unemployed and others. Undoubtedly, these groups experience specific hardships and problems with which social policy has to deal, but their situation also derives in large measure from a more general state of affairs brought about the societal policies of parties and governments.

Such policies, which are a major factor in the constitution, extension, or contraction of a body of social rights, themselves depend upon the conceptions of society and the social philosophies that guide the actions of political parties in their efforts to influence the course of events, either in government or in opposition. They do so in two particularly important respects; first, in relation to the structure and operation of the economy, and secondly, in respect of the degree of equality that should exist among citizens and residents.

Right-wing parties tend to regard society as a collection of individuals connected with each other primarily through contractual relationships such as exist in a private enterprise economy, which provides an underlying model for social relations. This conception, however, may be variously expressed; in an extreme form, inspired by a selective reading of Adam Smith, as the proposition uttered by a former British prime minister, that 'there is no such thing as society', or in a more qualified form in the notion of a 'social market economy'. It is always qualified, in another sense, by an insistence on the importance of the nation-state (that is to say, on the obligations of formal citizenship), and a distaste for dual citizenship. The emphasis on the individual and individual enterprise also entails an acceptance of a large degree of economic and social inequality, and again in the extreme case, hostility to what is called a 'dependency culture'; though in the post-war period such inequality has been mitigated, to a greater or lesser extent in different countries, by welfare provisions designed to benefit the very poor.

Left-wing parties, on the other hand, are more inclined to conceive the economy as a process of social production of goods and services of all kinds (both public and private), which should be regulated, and in some degree planned, for the benefit of all the inhabitants of a country, implying also a greater equality among these inhabitants. The welfare state is generally seen as an important equalising agency, but one which needs to be complemented by other, more socialist measures, including progressive taxation of wealth and income and public ownership of some vital areas of the economy. What is distinctive in the doctrines of left-wing parties is this recognition of the social nature of production, and the emphasis on the ways in which the social product should be distributed in order to provide a comfortable and decent life for all those who live in the society.

In the post-war period, however, the doctrines of many, if not all, conservative and socialist parties have undergone a gradual change, and various intermediate views have emerged, expressed in such conceptions as the 'mixed'economy', the 'social market economy', or the 'socialist market economy'. As a result the opposition between right-wing and left-wing parties is now less extreme than it was earlier in the twentieth century, in many European countries, although this has come about largely through the growing post-war influence of socialist parties and their success in establishing the basic framework of the welfare state. Nevertheless, a conflict persists, as Marshall noted, between the tendency of a capitalist market economy to produce greater inequality, and the tendency, and intention, of the welfare state to create greater equality. What has become less clear, in the policies of many socialist parties, as compared with the ideas expounded by Durbin at the end of the 1930s (above, p. 60), is the part that is to be played in achieving greater equality, or in the longer term an egalitarian society, by other measures, and in particular by public ownership and economic planning, both of which have social effects going far beyond those resulting from the extensive provision of welfare services. Socialist parties, during the past few decades, have withdrawn to a considerable extent from their historical commitment to public ownership and planning, partly in reaction against the experience of the state-socialist societies, partly under the influence of new doctrines extolling the virtues of private enterprise and free markets, and condemning the inefficiency of publicly owned enterprises and the irrationality of planning.

These doctrines, which I have referred to elsewhere as a new 'folklore of capitalism', have been influential beyond their deserts if we consider the real achievements of planning and public enterprise in much of Western Europe since the war (Bottomore 1990, Chapter 3), but they have raised important questions about how extensive public ownership should be and what kind of relationship between planning and markets could achieve at the same time optimum economic efficiency and a less unequal distribution of the social product. The situation confronting all political parties and social movements is, however, still more complex if we consider two other major issues which profoundly affect the present and future state of human rights on a world scale. One is the relationship between the industrial countries and the poorer, less-developed countries of the Third World; the other, the impact of economic growth, as it has been conceived and implemented since the war, on the natural environment.

As to the first question it may be argued that the post-war development of the industrial societies has been, to a considerable extent, at the expense of low-income and some middle-income countries, because the economic dominance of the former has enabled them to dictate the terms of trade, investment and aid.[19] It is also true, however, that the policies pursued by dominant groups, for their own enrichment, in poorer countries themselves, have often created a still greater dependence on the industrial countries and on multinational corporations, and have impeded economic development; while in some countries, and notably at present in some parts of Africa, the failure to control population growth has greatly increased the difficulties.[20] Since the early 1980s many studies have been devoted to what has become known as the North–

South divide (though this is geographically somewhat misleading),[21] but there have not yet emerged effective international policies which would reduce significantly the gap between rich and poor countries, or even prevent its widening; and for as long as this gap remains as wide as it now is, there will be gross inequalities in the extent of human rights, especially social rights, between different regions of the world.

The impact of economic development on the environment provokes equally important questions about social rights, affecting industrial, industrialising and non-industrial countries in various ways. The environmental costs of rapid industrialisation have been highlighted recently by the knowledge of its consequences in Eastern Europe which we have acquired since the revolutions of 1989, but the environmental damage inflicted by the capitalist industrial societies has also been very great, especially in the earlier phase of their development, and has been felt throughout large areas of the Third World as well as in the industrialised countries themselves. Only in the past two decades has such damage begun to be checked, through the actions of ecology movements and newly-formed green parties which challenge traditional conceptions of economic growth. But these new movements and parties still have difficulty in drawing support away from the older parties, and their main influence so far has been in modifying the policies of the latter to take more account of environmental issues.

It is evident today that what have been called the rights of citizenship, which I now refer to in a broader context as human rights, are in a continuous process of development which is profoundly affected by changing external conditions (especially in the economy), by the emergence of new problems and the search for new solutions. One major, more or less constant, factor in this process, as I have emphasised, has been the antithesis between the inegalitarian structure and consequences of a capitalist economy and the claims for greater equality made by diverse social movements since the end of the eighteenth century. Within this general opposition of different interests and values the conflict between classes and class-based parties still plays a leading role as a principal source of policies intended to limit or extend the scope of human rights, and in particular the degree of collective provision to meet what are defined as the basic needs of all members of a society at various stages in its development. Yet it is clear that in the late twentieth century other kinds of inequality besides those of class—between rich and poor countries, between the sexes, between ethnic groups—have become more salient than they were, even if in some cases they can be related, in part, to the inequalities engendered by capitalism.

Looking back to 1949 we can see that the discussion of rights at that

time was profoundly affected by a number of specific factors: the vivid
recollection of pre-war unemployment, poverty, inadequate health care
and education; the change in social attitudes brought about by the war,
and in particular the growing influence of the European socialist movement; and in Britain the commitment of the post-war Labour government
to overcoming the social evils of the 1930s, partly through the creation
of a welfare state, partly by more socialist measures, such as Durbin
(1940) had envisaged, in order to accomplish, by degrees, a radical
transformation of the economy and the class system. Marshall's essay
made a seminal contribution to this discussion by distinguishing between the three areas of civil, political and social rights, exploring the
relationship between them, and emphasising the increasing importance
of social rights in the twentieth century. In retrospect his study can be
seen as formulating some general principles for the welfare state, and as
foreshadowing to some extent the mixed economies of welfare capitalism which later emerged, while recognising the tensions that were likely
to persist in this form of society between egalitarian and inegalitarian
tendencies. These tensions became more acute in the late 1970s, and
Marshall, after having contributed substantially to studies of the welfare
state and its problems in successive editions of his book *Social Policy*
(1965, 5th edn, 1985), returned in an essay of 1981 (see above pp. 59–61)
to a consideration of the relation between capitalism, socialism and
welfare, in the course of which he asserted forthrightly that the mixed
economy was 'not enough', particularly in that sphere of policy which
is concerned with the prevention rather than the relief of poverty. Today,
Marshall's conception of citizenship is often invoked to stress the importance of civil and political rights, both in themselves and as means for
the extension of social rights–more particularly with reference to the
collapse of the communist dictatorships in Eastern Europe–but I do not
think he would have been at all enthusiastic about any sweeping
restoration of *laissez-faire* capitalism as an outcome of this collapse, and
he might well have looked with a sympathetic, if critical, eye on the
various projects for democratic 'socialism with markets' which aim to
create the kind of new social order, combining economic efficiency with
social justice, that he advocated.

It is from such a standpoint, at all events, that I have undertaken this
new analysis of the development of rights, in the spirit of Marshall's
essay, and endeavouring, as he did, to form new conceptions that may
help to illuminate the paths along which further progress is possible. But
in certain respects, as will be clear, I have diverged from his approach.
First, taking account of the very different issues that are raised by formal
and substantive citizenship, I have reached the conclusion that we

should examine civil, political and social rights in the framework of a conception of general human rights, rather than citizenship. I have also argued that human rights need to be considered on a global scale, above all in the context of the massive inequalities between rich and poor nations. Further, I have given more attention to ethnic and gender inequalities which coexist with those of class, and in some times and places are more prominent; but at the same time I have emphasised more strongly than Marshall did the historical role that classes, and the conflict between them, have played in limiting or extending the range of human rights. In the same context I have also argued that *all* human rights–civil, political and social–are continually developing and should not be regarded at any historical moment as having attained a final, definitive form. The social inventiveness of human beings seems to me as great as their capacity for technological innovation. Finally, I have emphasised perhaps more strongly than Marshall did the economic and class constraints upon the effective exercise of formally established rights, and from that perspective have attributed greater importance to a socialist reconstruction of the economy which would greatly reduce the concentration of wealth and economic power in the hands of a particular class.

The state of human rights in the world today, and their development, show contradictory features. In many countries the social rights embodied in the institutions of the welfare state have become less secure as a consequence of the economic recession, and in some cases, there has been a greater reliance on market forces rather than public expenditure.[22] At the same time the gap between rich and poor countries has steadily widened, and in the world as a whole poverty has been increasing. On the other side, the revolutions in Eastern Europe and the continuing reforms in the Soviet Union have established fundamental civil and political rights, although in the process some valuable social rights are being lost; while in Western Europe the proposed 'social charter' of the European Community is a notable attempt to extend the range of social rights. For Europe as a whole there is now a prospect, in this decade, of extending human rights in ways which encompass many of the new issues that I have discussed, but this will only come about, in my view, to the extent that social and societal policies are informed by a conception of social production as the planned production of welfare, or well-being, which entails also an equitable division of the product among the members of society. Over the longer term, policies are needed to achieve a more equitable distribution of the product of social labour on a world scale, and it is here, without doubt, that the most daunting and intractable problems have to be faced. The alternative to solving them, however, is the continued existence of a world riven by discord and conflict, in which islands of well-being are surrounded by oceans of misery.

Notes

1. On these different aspects see Tinbergen (1968), Van der Pijl (1989).
2. In Sweden almost continuously throughout the post-war period, and in Austria for much of the time since 1970.
3. See Panitch (1977), Offe (1980).
4. See Bottomore (1990, pp. 112–13, 130).
5. The differences between France and Germany are more extensively analysed in Brubaker (1992).
6. See A. Szalai (1972).
7. The most influential early study to raise these issues was probably Simone de Beauvoir's *The Second Sex* (1949), which was followed by a spate of publications from diverse standpoints, provoking many disagreements and controversies, for example between feminists and Marxists (Barrett 1988, Banks 1981).
8. The general pattern of change is indicated in a study of occupations in Britain by Routh (1980) who shows that between 1951 and 1979 the proportion of the occupied population classified as manual workers (including foremen) fell from 72 per cent to 54 per cent, while the proportion of clerical and professional workers, managers and employers rose from 28 per cent to 46 per cent (pp. 5, 45). By 1990 the proportion of manual workers had declined still further.
9. I have examined these and other aspects of the changing class structure more fully in Bottomore (1991).
10. I have referred elsewhere (Bottomore 1991, Chapter 5) to studies made in some other European countries.
11. For an account of the different attitudes and policies in some of these countries, see Gallie (1978), Scase (1977), Rydén and Bergström (1982). It should be noted too that in France since 1981 public ownership has been extended, while in Sweden the project for employee investment funds outlined a new conception of collective ownership (Bottomore 1990, p. 130).
12. They also point out, however, that these policies involved 'continued centralisation, bureaucratisation, intensified efficiency and a sense of alienation in the individual facing large private and public bureaucracies'; and these are matters to which I shall return later.
13. For a short survey of these doctrines, see Grant (1992), and for a critical analysis of them King (1987).
14. See the exposition of a project for European recovery from a socialist perspective in Holland (1983).
15. On one important aspect of this question, see Hirsch (1977).

16. But in Eastern Europe too there are opposing movements to create a broader federation, especially in the regions of central Europe which once formed part of the Habsburg empire, though the difficulties are formidable (Ash 1989). Furthermore, the admission of new member states to the EC, including some from Eastern Europe, which seems possible during the next decade, would extend the area in which federalist rather than nationalist structures prevail.

17. On the question of democracy and participation see Pateman (1970), and for a critical assessment Holden (1988, Chapter 3).

18. I use this term in the sense given to it by Ferge (above, p. 62).

19. Maddison (1989) has shown that between 1950 and 1987 the average GDP per capita in Latin America and Asia declined relative to that in the industrial (OECD) countries (although there was some improvement in Asia after 1973). Furthermore, in the 1980s an increasing number of countries, especially in Africa and Latin America, experienced an absolute decline in GDP per capita (see *Socialist Economic Bulletin*, 3, December 1990).

20. See the discussion by Myrdal (1968, vol. 2, part 6) in his study of poverty in South Asia, and more recently by Tabah (1982).

21. One of the best known is that produced by the Independent Commission on Development Issues, chaired by Willy Brandt, which gave wide currency to the North–South distinction (Brandt Commission 1983). See also the discussion of this and other reports by Holm (1985).

22. Some of the complexities and problems of the welfare state in Britain, which were already apparent in the 1980s, are indicated in Marshall (1985, in the concluding chapter by A.M. Rees).

Bibliography

Ash, Timothy Garton (1989) 'Does Central Europe exist?' in George Schöpflin and Nancy Wood (eds), *In Search of Central Europe* (Oxford: Polity Press/Blackwell).

Banks, Olive (1981) *Faces of Feminism* (Oxford: Martin Robertson).

Barrett, Michèle (1988) *Women's Oppression Today* (2nd edn; London: New Left Books).

Beauvoir, Simone de (1949) *The Second Sex* (Harmondsworth: Penguin Books, 1983).

Bottomore, Tom (1990) *The Socialist Economy: Theory and Practice* (Hemel Hempstead: Harvester-Wheatsheaf).

Bottomore, Tom (1991) *Classes in Modern Society* (2nd edn; London: Unwin Hyman).

Brandt Commission (1983) *Common Crisis, North–South: Cooperation for World Recovery* (London: Pan Books).

Braverman, H. (1974) *Labour and Monopoly Capital* (New York: Monthly Review Press).

Brubaker, W. Rogers (1992, forthcoming) *Citizenship and Nationhood in France and Germany* (Cambridge, Mass. Harvard University Press).

Brubaker, W. Rogers (ed.) (1989) *Immigration and the Politics of Citizenship in Europe and North America* (Lanham, New York, London: University Press of America).

Durbin, E.F.M. (1940) *The Politics of Democratic Socialism* (London: Routledge).

Ferge, Zsuzsa (1979) *A Society in the Making: Hungarian Social and Societal Policy, 1945–75* (Harmondsworth: Penguin Books).

Gallie, Duncan (1978) *In Search of the New Working Class* (Cambridge: Cambridge University Press).

Goldthorpe, John H. and Lockwood, David (1963) 'Affluence and the British class structure', *Sociological Review*, 11 (2), July.

Goldthorpe, John H. et al. (1969) *The Affluent Worker in the Class Structure* (Cambridge: Cambridge University Press).

Grant, R.A.D. (1992, forthcoming) 'The New Right', in William Outhwaite and Tom Bottomore (eds), *Blackwell Dictionary of Twentieth Century Social Thought* (Oxford: Blackwell).

Hilferding, Rudolf (1910) *Finance Capital: A Study of the Latest Phase of Capitalist Development* (London: Routledge & Kegan Paul, 1981).

Hirsch, Fred (1977) *Social Limits to Growth* (London: Routledge & Kegan Paul).

Holden, Barry (1988) *Understanding Liberal Democracy* (Hemel Hempstead: Philip Allan).

Holland, Stuart (ed.) (1983) *Out of Crisis: A Project for European Recovery* (Nottingham: Spokesman Books).

Holm, Hans-Henrik (1985) 'Brandt, Palme and Thorssen: A strategy that does not work?', *IDS Bulletin,* 16 (4), October (Brighton: Institute of Development Studies at the University of Sussex).

King, D. (1987) *The New Right: Politics, Markets and Citizenship* (London: Macmillan).

Lister, Ruth (1990) *The Exclusive Society* (London: Child Poverty Action Group).

Maddison, Angus (1982) *Phases of Capitalist Development* (Oxford: Oxford University Press).

Maddison, Angus (1989) *The World Economy in the Twentieth Century* (Paris: OECD).

Mallet, Serge (1975) *The New Working Class* (Nottingham: Spokesman Books).

Marshall, Alfred (1873) 'The future of the working classes', in A.C. Pigou (ed.), *Memorials of Alfred Marshall* (London: Macmillan, 1925).

Marshall, T.H. (1972) 'Value problems of welfare-capitalism', reprinted in Marshall 1981.

Marshall, T.H. (1981) *The Right to Welfare and Other Essays* (London: Heinemann).

Marshall, T.H. (1985) *Social Policy* (5th edn, completed by A.M. Rees; London: Hutchinson).

Marx, Karl (1844) 'Critique of Hegel's Philosophy of Right. Introduction'.

Myrdal, Gunnar (1968) *Asian Drama* (New York: Pantheon).

Offe, Claus (1980) 'The separation of form and content in liberal democratic politics', *Studies in Political Economy,* 3.

Panitch, Leo (1977) 'The development of corporatism in liberal democracies', *Comparative Political Studies,* 10(1).

Pateman, Carole (1970) *Participation and Democratic Theory* (Cambridge: Cambridge University Press).

Postan, M.M. (1967) *Economic History of Western Europe, 1945–64* (London: Methuen).

Renner, Karl (1953) *Wandlungen der modernen Gesellschaft. Zwei Abhandlungen über die Probleme der Nachkriegszeit* (Vienna: Wiener Volksbuchhandlung).

Report of the Royal Commission on Population, June 1949. Cmd. 7695. (London: Stationery Office).

Robson, William A. (1976) *Welfare State and Welfare Society* (London: Allen & Unwin).

Routh, G. (1980) *Occupation and Pay in Great Britain 1906–79* (London: Macmillan)

Rydén, Bengt and Bergström, Villy (eds) (1982) *Sweden: Choices for Economic and Social Policy in the 1980s* (London: Allen & Unwin).

Scase, Richard (1977) *Social Democracy in Capitalist Society: Working Class Politics in Britain and Sweden* (London: Croom Helm).

Schumpeter, J.A. (1942) *Capitalism, Socialism and Democracy* (6th edn; London: Allen & Unwin, 1987).

Schumpeter, J.A. (1949) 'The march into socialism' (an address to the American Economic Association, incorporated in later editions of *Capitalism, Socialism and Democracy*).

Socialist Economic Bulletin, 3, December 1990 (London).

Szalai, A. et al. (eds) (1972) *The Use of Time* (The Hague: Mouton).

Tabah, L. (1982) 'Population growth', in Just Faaland (ed.), *Population and the World Economy in the 21st Century* (Oxford: Blackwell).

Tawney, R.H. (1952) *Equality* (4th edn; London: Allen & Unwin).

Tinbergen, J. (1968) 'Planning, Economic (Western Europe)', in *International Encyclopaedia of the Social Sciences*, vol. 12 (New York: Macmillan and The Free Press).

Titmuss, Richard M. (1956) 'The social division of welfare: some reflections on the search for equity', in *Essays on 'The Welfare State'* (London: Allen & Unwin, 1958).

Titmuss, Richard M. (1962) *Income Distribution and Social Change* (London: Allen & Unwin).

Turner, Bryan S. (1986) *Citizenship and Capitalism* (London: Allen & Unwin).

Van der Pijl, Kees (1989) 'The international level', in Tom Bottomore and Robert J. Brym (eds), *The Capitalist Class; An International Study* (Hemel Hempstead: Harvester-Wheatsheaf).

Webb, Sidney (1989) 'Historic', in G. Bernard Shaw (ed.), *Fabian Essays in Socialism* (London: The Fabian Society and Allen & Unwin, 1931).

Index

15028856R00063

Printed in Great Britain
by Amazon.co.uk, Ltd.,
Marston Gate.